Follies
of a
Navy
Chaplain

by

Connell J. Maguire

To Edward (Sarge) and Elizabeth
whose hearts of gold inspire me

Connell Joe Maguire

Printed at:
Ted Weiss Printing
409 Bridgetown Pike
Langhorne, PA

Published by:
Chi Chi Press
PO Box 914
Maywood, NJ 07607
(800) 807-8265

ISBN 0-9727330-1-9

To my parents, brothers and sisters who endowed
me with love and humor.

Foreword

An unlikely chain of events led me to Joe Maguire and "Follies of a Navy Chaplain." In 1987 I attended a reunion of my father's outfit from World War II, trying to reconstruct the stories he told when I was a kid. I became interested in the story of a young lieutenant who was killed during the war, and whose name I remembered my father mentioning. In 1996, during a visit to Germany, I went to the village where the lieutenant was killed. There I met a German historian who told me of a spectacular battle between American bombers and German fighter planes that took place in the skies above a nearby town. The German historian, as a boy of 12, had captured a 19-year-old American navigator who bailed out of his plane. Many years later, the German and the navigator were reunited, and the seeds were planted for the Kassel Mission Memorial, a monument honoring those who were killed on both sides in the battle.

Kay Brainard Hutchins, who was a Red Cross girl during the war, lost a brother on the Kassel Mission. Several years ago I interviewed her and included her story in my book "9 Lives: An Oral History." Kay is a neighbor of Joe Maguire, and showed him a copy of the book. Joe contacted me, and asked for advice on publishing "Follies."

I suggested he send me a copy. He did, and after only a few pages I already was in love with it. I hope that you will have the same reaction.

Table of Contents

Two Butterflies

Why do I remember clearly that moment, one sunny day in Ireland when I was about five years old? Running to and fro, I strove to unite myself somehow with the joyful pirouettes of two butterflies. My mother and I were waiting for someone where the lane met the Glenties road. I totally forget for whom we were waiting, the main reason for our being there. I don't remember who arrived. Memory plays by its own rules. It decides, at times, to record things that our intellect would not deem as noteworthy, and it also erases what mind would retain. All in all, of course, memory is kind. Should we remember our hurts as vividly as when they afflicted us, we would all be loco. Memory smooths rough edges, and fits us nicely with rosy specs.

A country road as background may have aided memory that day. A road speaks promise, and it can mean good-bye. I am grateful, now, that memory chose to file that peaceful moment, a picture of my mother seated, facing the town, pensive, expectant, while I, worry free, jumped with the yellow dancers.

Life was all before me then, and if you will turn the pages, you will find that memory chose to record some of my foibles and flaws (some, because it is not a huge tome), some sad, but mostly funny events. Strange that laughter predominates. We do not view our lives as funny. But perhaps in retrospect or to a disinterested observer, our lives actually are funny.

This is true, however, only if we are among those who escape devastating tragedy. While you travel with me over miles and days, through war and peace from Ireland to Vietnam and back, our eyes and hearts cannot help witnessing that rain also falls into life and sadly for some, in torrents.

Moon Enlightenment

My brothers Pat and Barney were three plus and two years respectively older than I. Hence they were stronger, much better informed, superior beings to me in every way during my formative years. This produced a complex in me, a need to prove myself, to be accepted, respected, indeed to be singled out for praise. It's still in there. Religious writers urge us to practice humility, so I lived a lot of my life combating what I took for evil pride. Later I came to realize that those infected with pride care little about acceptance by those for whom they have disdain. Everyone, of course, has a desire to be accepted with dignity into the human family. But with me, it's a bit much. However, knowing where I am coming from has given me some relief from the pressing burden of earlier years, my struggle to reform.

This, my inordinate quest for status, got me into trouble early and often. One day, standing on a little hillock, called the Nows, with my two brothers, I boasted that I could throw a stone from there into the river, a few hundred yards away. My sister Annie was below us, making believe she was a teacher. She must have had a tough teacher model because she had a sally rod in her hand and was tapping rocks which she judged inattentive. Animated by brotherly scorn of my project, I let the stone fly. It flew little. It conked Annie on the head. Had I aimed at her, we would both have been saved by my inaccuracy, though my spirit would have been soiled. I can still see her running up the lane to the house crying and indignant, and I knew I was in deep trouble. My humiliation was forgotten, out-gunned by the dread of uproar and punishment. To paraphrase, showing off goeth before a fall. In spades, on this occasion, even though Annie did not even suffer a lump from my mighty toss.

Because I learned good things also from my brothers, I must credit them with teaching me more than just survival tactics. Pat was the elder of us three, very smart and our intellectual leader. Somehow the title "seat of wisdom" was used in reference to him, an encomium which, I do believe, was originally self-bestowed. At least he accepted it with delight as his due. Fittingly, he became a philosophy professor in California.

On one occasion, the budding professor raised our consciousness dramatically. We were observing the moon, an important fixture in country night travel and visiting. He stunned Barney and me by informing us that if the moon were down here close by, we would see that it is not the size of a plate as we thought, but that in reality it is as big as a cart wheel.

Afterwards, as I looked at the measurements of Uncle Barney's cart wheel, I was in awe of our universe, and my newly elevated state of awareness.

Scrig and the Sea

As children in Ireland, we lived in the midst of beauty and even then we knew it. A tiny river, teeming with aquatic life, ran along our land. Green fields were surrounded on all sides by mountains. Scrig mountain was close and fascinating, despite her ugly name. Tall, strong, silent, she seemed to contain the history upon which she had looked with equanimity ever since first human eyes looked up to her. She seemed to say, "You mortals are born, grow, struggle and die. I alone remain healthy and strong, watching your feeble course."

Scrig's slopes were easy to climb and so well worth the effort. The scenery below was gorgeous. Heather covered the plateau at the summit, and the blue waters of Lough Hanagh sparkled there brightly, silently. An intriguing tree-covered island lay at the center of the lake. Brian Friel fished there and made the lake famous in his play "Dancing at Lughnasa."

Two of my experiences on that mountain are unforgettable. One sunny day, we explored a rocky area behind a peak. The ground was too forbidding and too inaccessible to have ever been tilled or utilized by any except stray sheep seeking forage. We came upon a very large rock there on which there were pre-historic carvings. My feelings as I gazed on it defy expression. The same quiet sunshine that highlighted the inscription for us shone on those who chiseled it ages before. I felt as though nothing had happened in that quiet spot between the inscribing and my arrival. I felt vibrations of the presence of those pre-historic men, as if they had just left there, as if we had missed seeing each other by moments only.

I wondered what were they like. What thought did the stone express? Illiterate in their script, I could not know.

There is a place called Newgrange not far from Dublin. A burial mound there is five thousand years old, older than the Pyramids or Stonehenge. Though tourists and buses will distract you there, you may feel some of what I felt as you examine ancient tracings. They are at the entrance to one of the planet's oldest rooms into which the sun shines on December 21, each year.

My other memorable experience was future directed. From the top of Scrig,

I saw the sea, for the first time, some seven miles away. A white sand dune there was also a new sight. "Coming events cast their shadows before," Shakespeare said.. Perhaps he meant that the future was already implicit in existing causes. Perhaps he meant something mystical such as what I felt at that moment, that the sea was in my future.

Let's agree it was the former after all, that my fantasy was self-fulfilling. I was to spend twenty-six years in the United States Navy and sail on the sea in every time zone of the planet.

Fifty plus years after our childhood explorations of Scrig, we climbed that mountain again. Transfixed, I gazed at that far away sea scene with much older eyes. Like Scrig, it was just the same. Only I had changed.

While the Lord Fished

Tourists were allowed by the government to enter our farm and fish along the river bank. A no trespassing sign was a non-existent entity then. There was no resentment on the part of the farmers. These tourists brought money and employment to the area. For one thing each one hired a local gaffer to hook the salmon. They were company and excitement too, something different, from another world, dispelling country loneliness.

Occasionally a bicycling or hiking tourist would come and ask permission to camp near the river. No one thought of denying their request. If they wanted eggs or tea or other items, they paid. However, if on occasion they entered the house, tea was served as a treat.

I remember while we were living elsewhere and I was sent by my mother to "baby-sit" Grandma so she would not be lonely, a fisherman came and asked if he could come in for a cup of tea. He would be offering payment in that circumstance. Grandma made tea of record density, a veritable Tetley black hole. The man asked if he could have some hot water. Sitting quietly, observing the scene, I knew he wanted to lighten the tea. He got his hot water all right, but not before Grandma put a handful of tea in it. She interpreted his word as a bashful, gentle request for more tea. He graciously accepted his fate. Probably he didn't sleep that night.

A titled couple, a Lord and Lady, were the most memorable of tourists, especially the Lady. There was a write-up about them in the old Encyclopedia Britannica.

The Lady did not like to fish. She visited us and was delighted with the company of the three little boys. She bought us tennis rackets and showed us some tennis techniques. There wasn't a chance we would get to use them in soggy, poor Donegal.

The Lady told my mother she would give all the money in the world to have that darling little boy, Connell Joseph. My modicum of modesty and a need to fend off scorn prompts me to point out that all five-year-olds are adorable, most of the time. And I do concede that her appraisal was not widely shared in the neighborhood.

Two events involving the Lady I recall clearly, and I am intrigued by my reaction to them at such an early age. Perhaps they have a bearing on Jung's theory of the collective unconscious. His theory is borne out by the way similar feelings and ideas crop up around the world simultaneously in relatively unconnected areas. This can be observed in such things as inventions and medical breakthroughs which occurred even before our recent momentous development of communication.

You judge if these events were cases in point. The Lady took us aside one day to teach us how to address her. We were to say, "Yes, Your Ladyship" and "No, Your Ladyship." I had a strong feeling that she was doing something improper, even impolite, asking honors for herself. Had I come out of the ground with democratic sentiments, or had I been instructed along those lines by my family? I cannot dismiss the former.

The second instance is more clearly an out-of-the-ground phenomenon. The Lady, in our presence, gave my mother information Mam lacked and told her something she should do for us but was omitting. My mother, schooled in monarchical mores, which required respect for your "betters," registered no resentment. But I had negative feelings. I felt the Lady was bullishly usurping my mother's role, undermining her rightful place and authority, and embarrassing her in front of us. The feelings were there then. My analysis came later.

Not that the Lady was anything but kind, and desirous of helping us in every way. However, she operated according to standards which were in the process of changing worldwide. She was slightly anachronistic. Her goodness is not in question, but it is a paradox that she, an epitome of good manners in one era, should be, in a different age, counted as ill-mannered.

A little bull can be petted. They are like a large, beautiful dog. A grown bull is something else. Calloused by life's struggles and left brain training, I have lost much of the sensitivity to the feeling of others which I possessed, lopsidedly of course, as a child. I am less perceptive now.

Seventy plus years after the delightful Lady's visit, two ladies from Dublin visited the area where I live, Singer Island in Riviera Beach, Florida. We had a mutual friend in Dublin so they looked me up. They were close to my age and from the neighborhood of the Lady's castle. I asked if they knew her. Sure enough one said "Yes. I sat at the table with her at the golf club. She is dead now. She never had any children. She adopted a boy."

"Well, he was a second choice," I blurted.

From a chronological viewpoint, you must admit I was right. About attributes of quality, I can make no claim.

P.S. I was adorable.

Tom Gallen

Characters in a small town who would be jailed in a big city are often tolerated in a live-and-let-live spirit as long as they do no great harm and one can easily protect oneself. In a small town near where we lived, there was such a merry miscreant, the very man who invented womanizing. Tom Gallen will be his name. A woman entering his father's store had to keep moving and unhanding our tainted hero as she conducted her purchase. His humorous accounts of his escapades, often at his own expense, contributed to his survival. He certainly was not lacking in wealth of material.

The "Roaring Twenties" of the 20th century were not audible in Ireland. Ireland was poor and undeveloped, particularly our County Donegal and County Mayo from whence came most emigrants to America. We carried water from the well. There was no indoor plumbing or electricity. Chamber pots and the great outdoors served as toilets in country areas.

A young man from the country was in Tom Gallen's kitchen in town. The Gallens were relatively well off and owned a small hotel. The young man whispered to Tom that he needed to "loose a button," a euphemism for a bowel emptying. He started to go outside. Tom, of course, stopped him. "Right above the kitchen here there is a room where you can do that. You'll see where to sit." Shortly after there were shouts from above, sounding like a cocktail of curses and prayers. Tom rushed out. He met the young man on the stairs, gasping and white as a sheet.

"God save me, oh God I pulled on a wee chain and the whole charge went down into the kitchen."

On another occasion, our Tom regaled Johnny the blacksmith with an account of life in Mesopotamia.

"I was out there in the British army and that's where we should be, Johnny. Every man there has five women."

"You don't say," said Johnny open-mouthed. They were outside Johnny's house where he lived with his sister, known for her loud high-pitched voice.

"But the problem is," continued Tom, "that the mosquitoes are bad out there."

"Sure that's nothing at all," retorted Johnny with impassioned yet balanced logic. "Sure the midges have the ass eaten off us here and we only have one woman."

Johnny went inside the half-door which served to keep chickens out and Tom heard him inform his sister of the wonders of Mesopotamia.

"Don't you be listening to that Tom Gallen," came a voice all the village could hear. "Don't you know that if it was like that out there, Tom Gallen would never come back here."

The Cow and the Velvet Suit

My brothers had little difficulty persuading me to do daring and incongruous deeds. As young and old everywhere, we delighted in stories of American cowboys and Indians of the Wild West. One day Barney and I, pedestrian cowboys, were herding one cow along the road. Sod was piled up at roadside to serve as a dirt wall. A "shuhh" is a drainage ditch in Donegal. So the digging operation served two purposes and, on this day, a third. Grass grew profusely on the dirt wall and the cow paused to graze. Barney said, "This is your chance to be a cowboy. You can climb up beside the cow and ride on her back." I can still see the backbone of the cow, her silky, tan hair, as I climbed up and stretched my right leg across her midsection. No horse ever dashed from a gate faster than that uncooperative cow darted from underneath me, leaving a prospective cowboy rolling flat in the mud. I don't understand cows.

That was a closed case. No harm was done for which I would be held accountable. It was a different matter in the case of the velvet suit.

My mother was a dressmaker, and when I was between four and five, she made me a velvet suit with short pants. Out playing one hot day while I was wearing my new apparel, my brothers convinced me that it could double as a bathing suit. It was one of those days when the Irish say the "sun is splitting the rocks," all the while they are wearing sweaters and probably long underwear. I entered the river where it flowed over a shallow, stony bed. A surprising number of details of that misadventure are vivid in memory. I noted with interest that water rose higher on either side of me and that the stones were all rounded like eggs. Centuries of flowing water had given them this oval shape. I was delighted by how it all felt.

Suddenly, shouting from the house intruded on my new found pleasure. My brothers hauled me ashore and dragged me along to my judicial hearing. How could being wet in the river feel so good, and now walking in wet clothes feel so miserable? No one had an interest in answering that question. And why was my mother making such a big deal out of such a simple and happy matter? Probably the suit, fruit of much loving effort, was ruined. What happened to it after that is not recorded in family history.

Grandma's Strange Remorse

My grandfather Patrick Gallagher, a tall strong man, came back to Ireland from America in 1880, married Bridget Boyle, and took over the little family farm. He had been in the United States eleven years and was an American citizen. He and his cousin traveled the Carolinas and Virginia in the seventies selling a variety of wares. That would make them "Carpetbaggers."

He and his wife reared nine children, and he used to say proudly, "None of them gave me any trouble." But they gave him sadness. My mother remembered him at the end of the lane, saying to his eighteen-year-old son, "Good-bye Johnny forever." Physically sick from grief, he spent two days in bed. My mother recalled his placing her little sister Mary in her coffin, tears streaming down his cheeks. Mary got blood poison from a nail in her shoe. She had been preparing for First Communion. Because of her sore foot, my mother carried her in the lane the day she was tested. "I answered all the questions," she said. But she did not go out the lane for Holy Communion. A Father Boyce brought the sacrament to her at home, and she went out the lane in her coffin.

Grandma went through all that too. Four sons and two daughters left for America. We watched her often as she went out the lane to meet the postman, eager for a letter from her beloved.

Old people acted and were treated differently in those days. They were cared for at home but were treated as out of it. Their opinions were not given much credence and they were not consulted on family matters. Their day was over. Though I believe this was a general condition, perhaps it was more so in our family because of my grandmother's health and disposition. She was not always easy to get along with, she was high-strung, sickly and spent much time in her room. She loved poetry and music which she would hum softly by the fire. She came from a more industrious family than she had spawned. So I remember her calling to Uncle Barney from her room that neighbors were already out in the fields. Uncle Barney preferred carting to work in the fields. He liked hauling and meeting people in town and on the road. His horse was useless to others. Dad borrowed it for his delivery of bread to Ardara, a nearby town. As he was accustomed to, the horse stopped solid in his tracks whenever he met a person on the road, a service provided for Uncle Barney's social life. This distressed my father who was in a hurry to get to Ardara. And besides, my father wanted nothing less than gabbing with any and every pedestrian.

Uncle Barney was the only one of the nine still there when Grandma died.

I cherish letters she wrote to us after we emigrated to America. I marveled at the wisdom of someone who had never traveled outside the county. She was glad that our family was now all together, that the many separations before we went to the United States were over. In one of her letters she wrote, "I see the children on the upper road going in to school, but I miss my own wee boys." She was referring to Pat, Barney and myself. That love was unexpressed before.

I am sure we annoyed her often and much. One day she was raking the new mowed hay in the field and we three boys were wrestling and playing and getting in her way. She tapped me with the wooden rake to get me to move. It was a light touch. I felt no pain at all. But Grandma left off raking and went into the house. I remember distinctly her sitting by the fire, crying about the incident as she confessed it to my mother. I was amazed at the fuss over nothing. I deserved much more correction and I knew it. I was touched by this insight into my Grandmother's soul.

Wisdom of the Thorn

As a child,
To partake more of her beauty,

I plucked the rose.
I coaxed and cared for her
She faded and died.

Lacking restraint,
I did not heed the thorn,

"Love her, yes, but stay apart
Grasping is two edged

Learn from my advice
Accept
The unattainable in beauty"

Tale of a Donkey

It took a donkey, a jackass of all "people," to dissipate the aura of infallibility which, in my mind, surrounded my two brothers. Our animal loving Uncle Barney had bought an untrained and very independent donkey which he grazed on a vacant farm. There were "No trespassing" signs to be seen anywhere in our environs in those days. We trespassed there to our hearts' content petting and trying to ride the untamed donkey.

One day my Aunt Bridget needed turf (peat) for the fire. My two brilliant brothers decided to take the donkey to the bog to have him carry the turf. They borrowed a collar and reins and two creels from a neighbor, Ambrose Sweeney. Such creels are designed to hang one on either side of the jackass.

They started off on the narrow main road. The boys were very light so the donkey did not signal any opposition to their riding on him. He knew us by now. However, he insisted on taking the middle of the narrow road even in the face of an oncoming bus. The boys pulled the reins expecting the donkey to turn in the direction his head was pulled. But with his head sideways, the donkey kept going straight ahead as before. The brothers, in a frenzy, alighted and began pushing the donkey to the side of the road. They expected an outburst of annoyance, to say the least, from the bus driver and passengers, but they noticed that instead they were all laughing heartily.

Onward they proceeded down the Mullantboyle Lane. They went along fine until they came to a sharp turn in the lane. They pulled on the rein for a right turn, but the donkey turned only his head. He was now looking to the side but marching straight ahead in an unseen direction, right into the hedge.

Eventually they got to the bog and loaded the donkey while he dined on grass. A bog is a bog and after a few steps the loaded donkey's legs were submerged up to his belly. The burden was removed and the donkey was brought to solid ground. As they returned along the lane, their self-confidence received another blow. The McNamees were outside and pointed out gleefully that the collar on the poor donkey was on backwards.

Thanks, donkey. And my brothers could be wrong about Santa Claus too, I decided. "Why would grownups make pictures of him if he did not exist?" said I to my friends with new confidence.

The mind-of-his-own donkey could teach college students as well as me. Keep enough independence and have enough confidence to judge the attitudes, opinions and facts presented by your professors, even though you have to be civil to pass. You may agree with them later. That may make life duller. My Christmas became so when I agreed with my brothers about Santa Claus.

I love donkeys.

Milk Can Afield

We were living in the house my father built, where my sister Kathleen was born, about a mile or so from my Grandmother's home. We had no cow. Pat and I were sent to Grandma's for a can of milk. We agreed, with what proved to be a shallow spirit of harmony, that each of us would carry it half-way. Had we returned home by way of the road, we could have measured our duty by telegraph poles. However, we considered it more sensible to take a more direct shortcut through the fields. Pat carried first and reached a spot he said was half-way. Who was I to contradict the seat of wisdom? I did. I pointed out that a spot about ten paces farther on was half-way of the mile walk. Pat put the can down and would not take it any farther. I would not pick it up unless he did. Had we known the art of compromise, would it have helped? I doubt it. The can would not have been picked up by what my aunt called Pat, the stubborn gentleman.

So we went on home empty-handed and the pail of milk sat in the field, fodder for ants and flies. My mother asked, "Where is the milk?" She received oblique answers. Pat replied, "Joe wouldn't take it half-way."

"Well, where is the milk?"

"Pat wouldn't take it half-way."

By a series of questions my mother reached outrage, realizing that the milk was sitting in Friel's bog. Pat was three plus years older than I. "Go back you and get the milk. You are old enough to have better sense."

I was overdosed with justice. All I wanted was fairness. My unease however was not strong enough for even slight heroism. I did not protest that the judgment was excessive in my favor. More probably, I felt I was due a victory.

Pat and I went to Ireland a few years ago, two retired old codgers. His friends in California wanted a picture of us at the spot where we left the can of milk some 70 years ago. A neighbor there obliged. I said, after looking from one house to the other, "Look, Pat. It wasn't half-way." "Yes, it was," quoth he. Fortunately, this time there was no milk can.

The Ambush

One day in 1922, we were sitting outside enjoying rare Irish sunshine with visitors. One relative, Mamie Crowe, on whose knee I was sitting, died recently in Port Charlotte, Florida, at a ripe old age but still sprightly in disposition. She had married an Englishman named Kelly. There are such.

The guerrilla-type war for Irish independence had been going on for six years. I remember that day watching a double-decker lorry full of Black-and-Tans, the name ascribed to English soldiers, going out the main road. Moments later, bullets were swishing through the trees. My mother hustled me into the house as our white horse ran wildly toward us. Either he was frightened by the unusual noises or nipped by a falling bullet. The British had been ambushed from a stone wall overlooking a turn in the road. Fortunately for the people whose houses were within sight of the scene, the treaty between Ireland and England came through the next day. Otherwise they would have been held responsible and their houses wrecked.

Winston Churchill had offered Michael Collins a deal, hard to swallow, but which he could not sensibly refuse. The English would permit an Irish Free State composed of 26 of Ireland's 32 counties. The other six of the nine counties in the province of Ulster, now called Northern Ireland, would remain under English control. The majority of the people in the north were descendants of settlers brought into Irish lands (including the Maguire lands) after former failed revolts. These people were fiercely loyal to England and bitterly opposed to union with the rest of Ireland with whom they also differed religiously.

Churchill pointed out that there was no chance that the English parliament would agree to let these six counties go. Besides, postwar England could now flood Ireland with troops so Collins "could not move a bicycle." The English, too, were under pressure from world opinion to settle. American sympathy for freedom and self-determination of small nations, a popular idea after World War I, played a role, as did American partiality for the cause of Irish independence.

Collins knew, however, that his troops back in Ireland wanted total freedom for all of Ireland. Those with very strong feelings would be furious. Indeed as he signed the treaty, he said he was signing his warrant of death.

He was right. Civil war ensued between those who rejected and those who accepted the treaty. Collins' forces were backed by England and won. The opponents were outlawed but took with them the name Irish Republican Army, formerly the name of Collins' forces. Collins, however, as he foretold, was killed in the Civil War at age 33; Ireland's great hero was considered a traitor by the die-hards.

Collins has a place in world history. A mere youth, he had split the base of the British Empire, setting the stage and pattern for its dissolution. His method, actually named for him, was copied and used in the struggle of the Israelites for a homeland, and later by Mao Tse Tung.

As a by the way, when you fly into Dublin today, you are in Collins Airport.

Liam Neeson played the role of Michael Collins in the movie and Julia Roberts was his bride never-to-be.

EPILOGUE

Neither Collins nor Churchill could possibly have envisioned all the implications of the items on which they felt forced to agree, how these, in future history, would affect both nations. Collins was getting more for Ireland than the treaty granted, whereas Churchill was placing in incubation forces that proved to be negative for Britain. Rather than just an Irish Free State with Commonwealth status, an Irish Republic was soon to be born. But Churchill had agreed to the first crack in the British Empire, and at its base, as has been noted.

The pressure on Churchill and the English government was not Irish fighting power in itself, although the English people were tired of war and hostility. A more powerful antagonist was world opinion which favored the Irish in their struggle for independence. The inspiration of the movement for freedom was very articulately expressed. In addition to W.B. Yeats' writings, those executed in the 1916 rising were all published poets. The pen was mightier than the sword.

We can ask now, would Churchill, in the face of world opinion, have gone ahead with a massive military suppression of the revolution had he known the consequences of the treaty for the empire? Would he have counted on the world to forget and acted forcefully to save the empire? We will never know.

The Holy Mission's
Ill-Befitting Close

Tinkers, as they are called in Ireland, are something of a mystery. They are homeless by choice. Ireland has very little defense spending so the poor can get free housing, shopping service, meals, and laundry service. If you are either rich or poor you have it made in Ireland. The tinkers, sometimes called travelers, could have jobs now while the Irish economy roars ahead. They prefer their nomadic lifestyle. While they pile up trash along the roads, they do odd jobs and also receive charitable help from Irish homes. That tradition of kindness to them goes back to the days of landlord Boycott, whose name became a verb in our language. People were evicted and their houses leveled at the whim of the landlord. Social structures to come to their aid were lacking. They begged or got passage to America. In England, industry absorbed many of those evicted there. Boycott was the first landlord to bear the brunt of outrage. People refused to sell him anything, buy anything from him or work for him. Laws were passed in England to try to suppress this movement as it spread throughout Ireland. Relief finally came to Ireland under the land reform program of Prime Minister Gladstone. So Eugene O'Neill's second name is Gladstone in honor of Ireland's benefactor.

So much for prologue to my story of one tinker in distress. Our man was terribly hung over and arose late in the day in miserable condition. He set out hoping with all his being for a hair of the dog that bit him, at least one good shot of whiskey. He had no money, only trust that some kind soul in town would treat him. To this hope he was destined to add an expression of faith, but not yet. The town was shut tight. No pub was open. An old lady informed him that they were all up at church for the closing of the Holy Mission, a two- or three-week religious revival. Was God against him too? Perhaps the reverse was true. Some soul would be inspired to generosity by religious observance and would buy him a shot. So he hurried to church and found a seat at the back.

The congregation began to renew their baptismal vows led by the priest. The priest states the questions and the people answer "I do" as in a marriage ceremony. There is a modicum of silence between the "I do" and the next question, usually. But the tinker was a beat behind with his affirmation. When the priest phrased the question, "Do you renounce Satan?" and the people answered "I do," our man filled the church and the silent interval with a very loud "I do, the bastard."

There could be no doubt where he stood. He was with the program four square. Was he not proved worthy of a shot?

The Angelus and Uncle Dan

There are times when Uncle Dan's behavior was less than angelic, times when his prayers may have caused frowns rather than smiles in celestial circles. In the teen years of the twentieth century, Ireland was very poor. Workers in the bog did not wear wrist watches. How did they know at a distance from home when to quit and return home for supper? The Angelus bell would ring about six o'clock. The scene of people saying the Angelus prayer in the field is immortalized by Millet's painting. It took me a while to realize what a Japanese banker was telling me about it. He was saying that in the islands off Kyushu, where Christianity had survived in spite of the persecution of the seventeenth century, you could see living replicas of "MIRRAY'S" painting. The Japanese transforming of "L's" into "R's" confused me.

Despite outward appearances, Uncle Dan was not a true model of the painting. As a teenager, he was restless in the lonely bog and found the work boring. The man who hired him on as his helper was deaf. So, much earlier than at quitting time, Uncle Dan devoutly removed his cap, made the sign of the cross, and I suppose, recited the prayer. The deaf employer followed suit and home they went. The "DIVIL," my mother chuckled when she heard of it.

Some day I hope to find out how Uncle Dan's prayer fared above. I suspect the Lord chuckled too and gave him credit.

Eggs and the Man

In addition to his bent for speculation of a philosophical nature, Pat was also something of an entrepreneur. On one occasion, however, a budding venture was nipped early. Pat must have reasoned that since chickens of little talent, tepid temperature and much covering could hatch eggs, why not he? He took an egg to bed for that purpose, a bed he shared with me. In a very short time, the egg was splattered on the bed and Pat was roaring crying, and accusing me of having pushed him. My mother came up the stairs to investigate the uproar. She remembers seeing me, looking over the sobbing body, with fear in my eyes as to what judgment awaited me, the accused cause of it all. Mam cleaned up the mess, did not accept testimony against me, and calmed Pat down with the promise that she would get him lots of eggs to hatch later on in the vacation.

Pat's enthusiasm for his project did not decline. In the interlude, we were outside one day as Father Logue was passing reading his prayer book. He stopped and Pat right away regaled him with prophecy of the great event soon to come.

"But wouldn't you break the egg?" the priest asked.

Pat got down on the grass and curled up to show how this would not happen. Pat didn't see but I noticed that my mother and Father Logue were giggling furiously. They are missing the point, I thought. His weight would not be on the egg. I was missing the point of a young man lying on the grass demonstrating how to hatch an egg.

Days passed and Pat suddenly realized that vacation and hatching time were getting short. He confronted my mother: "You promised me eggs to hatch and we will soon be going back to school. I need them right away."

"Well now Pat," my mother said, "you see how the little chicks follow the mother hen everywhere she goes after they are hatched. The other boys will think it funny to see you in the school yard with little chickens following you everywhere you go."

This raw use of peer pressure brought a sudden halt to the noble but for me, his bedmate, disturbing experiment.

A few years ago, Pat sent me a clipping from a California (where else?) paper, the obituary of a woman who had performed the same experiment as an adult and claimed success. "I was just ahead of my time," said Patrick sadly.

St. Patrick Gets the Blame

In case you are not a New Yorker, St. Patrick is the patron saint of Ireland and his feast day is March 17. In Ireland this day is observed as a holy day and, as on a Sunday, Catholics are required to attend Mass. Nobody came in a car in the early 1900s. Most walked, some many miles to the village church. In our town we had no parades. It was strictly a religious celebration until it reached the pub door. Then it became mixed. Friends who hadn't seen each other all winter were delighted to meet in a cozy setting and to "drown their shamrocks" with a drop of the "crather." You guessed it.

Who was this St. Patrick? As a boy, he was captured by Irish raiders and brought to Ireland as a slave. From where? Most likely Great Britain. He was a Catholic and since England was not yet Christian, he was undoubtedly from a Roman military or civil service family. Romans were still there in the 400s. However, that does not prove that he was of Italian ancestry. For now let Italians be satisfied with Columbus Day. The Romans often hired civil servants from conquered areas. But the name PATRICIUS is definitely Roman. So Italians are justified in lifting a green beer or Guinness that day.

The slave Patrick escaped from Ireland some years later, went to the continent and became a priest. He wanted to return to pagan Ireland as a missionary. He could have served and been a good priest on the continent. He owed nothing to the Irish, who had treated him cruelly. If that had been the size of his heart, he would have been buried in an unknown grave. His was one of the greatest acts of forgiveness in history. Convinced he had much to give the Irish, he returned in 432. His forgiveness led to great accomplishments. I measure his influence from a religious point of view. He was one of the most successful missionaries of all time. He succeeded in christianizing a whole nation in his lifetime. He was both zealous in faith and a genius in organization. No small task to change the minds of stubborn Irishmen.

Others may rejoice in St. Patrick's big-hearted mercy for other reasons, appalled by what life would be without green beer and parades and New York's

St. Patrick's Cathedral. By the way, St. Patrick's Cathedral in Dublin is a Protestant church.

George Gobel told a joke about Ireland that was well received at the time. What Irish event happened in 432 that changed history? You would expect an answer "St. Patrick returned to Ireland." "No," said George, "whiskey was invented to keep the Irish from ruling the world." A politician told that same joke recently only to discover that ethnic jokes get one in trouble now, in this our roots conscious era.

So much for the praise. What of the blame St. Patrick endured? It all happened on the good saint's feast day. It involves a devout lady whose full name I will withhold even though the incident dates back to my father's youth.

Kate had trudged the county road to attend Mass on St. Patrick's day and to sing hymns in his honor. Then she was delighted to meet her recently hibernated friends to enjoy a warm afternoon in the pub together. It gets dark early in winter and early spring in Ireland, since Ireland is as far north as northern Canada. The roads were unlighted and Kate on her way home, handicapped by the darkness, etc., failed to navigate a curve, and fell into the ditch, a "shugh" in Donegal. As my father and other young boys were extracting her from her muddy experience she moaned over and over "O holy Saint Patrick. What I am suffering for you."

Uncle Donal to the Rescue

Uncle Donal died before I was born. Actually he was my great uncle, Grandpa's brother. He was a retired postman, a happy servant of Queen Victoria's government which ruled Ireland. The postman walked in those days. Donal had scorn for his nephew Patrick who rode a bicycle. Uncle Donal may have had "a drop taken" once too often or perhaps he was just senile. He lived with my mother's parents in his declining years. There are many tales about his exploits and some of his aphorisms became part of our household lingo, some allowed only in jest as they were abrupt to say the least. Grandma tried to force him to eat. His most famous response was "Give it to your own hungry beagles." I never knew the proper pronunciation of "beagle," because in County Donegal the "ea" as pronounced "AE." Tea was tae. The beagles in this case were Grandma's beloved children. Uncle Donal liked sheep and usually had just two roaming the hills. He sold them before the cold weather. He referred to this transaction as "I rid my hand for the winter." That saying still serves many family actions. The man who bought the two sheep was then treated with what had been his own money and Uncle Donal "rid his hand" a second time.

Once, in his prime, he was delivering letters to a house in Fanat which was surrounded by police preparing a raid. The family were justly suspected of making "poteen," an illegal and powerful whiskey. Uncle Donal entered the home, delivered the letters, put the illegal poteen in the mail bag and marched forth. Perhaps the police saw a bulge in the mail bag. Maybe Uncle Donal's reputation was enough to arouse suspicion. Whatever the motive, the police captain called out "Search the postman." Sturdy Uncle Donal raised his hand. "No, no," he said. "You may not touch Her Majesty's mail." He hid the whiskey, returned it later and received a just though tainted reward.

The Muslim Burial

A little orientation is needed in vocabulary and geography for appreciation of this event in Glenties. The term "chance it" in Ireland means to take a chance. You may have guessed that. It can be used in combination with "Let's" or "We'll," etc.

I do not know the precise location of the town of Doohery, but I believe in its existence. On a desolate stretch of road through bog land between Glenties and Letterkerry, I once saw an old wooden sign pointing to Doohery. Also there is a song "Oh to be in Doohery," the ecstasy of whose message I have yet to experience. The song may be about the same Doohery. This story also gives credence to the importance of Doohery.

Now to our account of that solemn occasion. Would that I could repeat it for you as a classmate in Ireland, Thomas Brennan, present there at the time, related the incident to me. You may see a moral in the tale. Perhaps you will glean that efficiency goes into reverse if overdone, or that while projecting a good image one must beware of undesirable side effects.

The story begins with the sadness of some unknown person or persons. During World War II a body, identified as a Muslim, was washed ashore on a beach near Glenties. Evidently he also had on his person the name and address of his next of kin. Due to the war, he could not be shipped home. He would have to be buried in Ireland, a rare occurrence for a Muslim.

The minister from a nearby town took charge of arranging a proper burial. He came and instructed two burly local men, whom Thomas Brennan could name, that the deceased must be buried facing Mecca, and indicated how this was to be accomplished. The diggers agreed to carry out the somber task devoutly. However, this simple denouement was not to be.

The consulate of the man's country saw a need to become closely involved. An official came down from Derry to exercise a hands-on direction of the interment. The plan was that he could then return and write to the grieving family of how properly and respectfully he had visited the grave site and supervised proceedings.

But oh the perils of bureaucracy.

The diggers were of course awe-stricken in the presence of this well-dressed man from the city representing some exotic far-off land. After instructing them on the direction of Mecca he left, but first he gave them a generous tip of five pounds, quite a lot at that time. Several motives contributed to their next series of actions. They had felt strain while talking with this august stranger. Also, it was now the hottest part of the day. They had five pounds to spend which their wives knew not of. They were thirsty. Strongly motivated, they went off into town to relax and down a few Guinnesses. Dutifully they returned later to the cemetery to do the job. Let's call them Pat and Mike. Mike outlined the direction of the grave and started digging.

Pat shouted, "What are you doing man?"

"What we're supposed to do. Point the man toward Mecca, toward that tree over there."

"That's not what the man said at all, at all. He said the grave has to face the whin bush over there."

"Nonsense. Sure I was standing next to him."

The confidence of each man was being eroded by the other. After much discussion, doubt, and head scratching, Pat concluded, "We'll point him toward Doohery and chance it."

The Prize Turkey

The last dastardly deed of Pat and Barney on Erin's Green Isle, they classified as top secret. There was a turkey which was Aunt Bridget's pride and joy, a beautiful bird. She talked often of entering him in a show. She was sure of winning. One day when she was in the town, Pat and Barney tied a can on a string and the string to the turkey's leg. The turkey ran in vain in a frenzy to get away from whatever noisy entity was behind her. Round and round the outside of the house she went, feathers flying at every corner. For some reason, known only to chickens and their psychologists, the chickens all ran after her. By the time she was exhausted, she was bald in many parts. When Bridget next eyed the turkey she exclaimed, "Some terrible disorder came on her." I am not sure whether "disorder" was a generic term or a specific diagnosis.

Years later, when we were more bald than the turkey, Barney and I returned to visit our old home, twenty-one years after leaving to be exact. Barney spoke to me about the turkey, but he still could not face up to confessing to Aunt Bridget what was the source of the great "disorder."

Mullantboyle

I raced the lanes
Picked the flowers
Visioned heroes of old
On surrounding hills
And wondered at it all

From a world that changed me
To a world unchanged
With sparse grey hair
And dearth of teeth
I return

To walk the lanes
Commune with flowers
Glimmer the landscape
* with memories*
And wonder at it all
Again

Farewell

My parents had a shop and a good business in Glenties town at the time of the Irish war for independence from England. However, there was not much opportunity for young people. My mother had witnessed her four brothers leave for America, never to return to their grieving parents. She dreaded that fate. She saw boys, fresh from school, sitting on the corner smoking. Something had to be done and soon. There were four children then and taking us to America would be a chore and expensive. They had relatives in Scotland so there we went to Greenock, the Brooklyn of Scotland. I was just a year and a half so I do not remember the bonny, bonny banks of Loch Lomond. The expedition to Scotland did not work out so back we came to Mam's grandparents. Dad left for America to make a living for us. He went back and forth over a period of nine years. In 1923, he built a house in Ireland and tried to find work there. Kathleen was born in December in that house. We went to Yeats County where Dad had some friends but no luck. Dad had to leave again. Finally in 1928, Mam took Kathleen and went to check out the possibility of taking the whole family to America. She left Barney, Pat, and me with Aunt Bridget in the new house. Anne was in boarding school in County Monaghan.

Mam returned in 1929. Teresa was born in June and varicose veins laid Mam up for days. Later she sold the house for the fare to America, and hired a car and driver to take the six children to Dublin to the American Embassy for physical exams and processing. I remember a stenographer asking another should she describe my hair as black or brown. What's left is neither now. We sailed from Belfast. The ship was a day late so they put us up in a hotel. I don't recall street cars in Dublin. I do remember being stunned to think how expensive concrete roads and streets must be as we approached Dublin. In Belfast we watched the trolleys together until I was scornfully excluded when I remarked I hadn't yet seen any trolleys on the middle two tracks. We landed in New York just after the ominous stock market crash, soon to affect us. My father was on the pier to meet us. Then and for many years, I took for granted all my parents did for us.

Almost all the news about the United States that made the Irish, English and Scottish papers was about gangsters and kidnaping. I had the impression that other than the Irish and the rich Americans who hired the Irish, all other Americans were gangsters and kidnappers. I promptly received a scare. I had lagged behind the others carrying a suitcase. A man grabbed me by the arm. My God, I didn't last five minutes in this country. I shouted "Mam! Mam!" I still wonder why he stopped me.

So much had happened in a short time. That independent recorder within me was at work all the while, clicking some moments into memory's file and erasing others.

For our last months in Ireland, we had moved from my grandmother's house to a house on a rise in a field in Meenahalla. Perhaps there was friction with five children, my mother expecting, my uncle and grandmother all in one house. We had a grand time in the rented house, kicking a football around the field and exploring the huge stone remains of a rath, a prehistoric burial mound. A row house in Philadelphia would be quite different. So would plumbing and electricity and an instant gas "fire" in the morning that saved so much time.

My mother did not go down to Mullantboyle that morning of our departure to say goodbye to her mother. She was busy with a five-month-old baby, luggage and checking on the other four of us. Besides, the Irish do not like to say goodbye.

The night before many neighbors came to say farewell, to try to enliven the traditional "American wake" the night before emigrants departed forever. How different all this is now!

Of that morning, a few things are etched clearly in memory. I was delegated to take a hammer back to Uncle Barney at my grandmother's. I don't remember whether I saw either one of them. I never saw Grandma again. I had to walk the equivalent of a block on the main road on my way with the hammer. I met the McNamees going into town to our school, this time without us. We didn't hug or say goodbye. We took the meeting in stride as just another happening. But that something in me wrote it down indelibly. Our worlds were separating. We would never see each other again. I did not feel it then.

I remember combing my hair in front of a little brown framed mirror. I forget how we got to the station. Rose Kennedy in a khaki raincoat was the only one to see us off. She said she too would emigrate. She never did. My mother and sister were crying as the train pulled out. My brothers were sad. I wasn't. To me it was an adventure.

Dad Loses His Job

The Stotesbury estate was to play a large role in our lives. My father worked there when we came to America. Mr. Stotesbury was the richest man in the Philadelphia area, a partner of J.P. Morgan. There were a hundred bedrooms in the house, all furnished at ultimate expense. The ballroom was gymnasium size. What a library! Volumes of famous writers, in their original languages, and beautifully bound. I worked there waxing floors one summer. How I enjoyed sitting in that expansive library, so quiet because of the miles of fields and gardens surrounding the dwelling. The gate house, two miles from the main house, still stands on Willow Grove Avenue in Wyndmoor. At a time when heads of families worked for fifteen dollars a week, if they worked at all, my father made thirty-five, enough for the survival of seven children, and for my mother's passion to save a little for a "rainy day."

Dad and Campbell Greer became friends at Stotesbury and eventually so too did my mother and Mabel Greer. We and the Greers became a united family. That seemed strange to many since we were Roman Catholic. Mr. Greer was North of Ireland Presbyterian, and Mrs. an Episcopalian. It was said Mr. Greer knew the Bible better than the minister. He was strict with himself but very sweet, gentle and tolerant of others. As did many Scottish people, Mrs. Greer loved music and dancing. One Sunday evening when Campbell Greer was expected, Mrs. Greer was dancing while Dad played the violin. Campbell did not approve of dancing, especially on a Sunday, because dancing led to the beheading of John the Baptist. He did not come in, but he did not criticize or try to impose his outlook on the rest of us.

At the time our families met, the pall of the big depression darkened life in America. We changed trolleys at Broad and Erie on our way to school, and men stood there behind little pyramids of apples. They looked forlorn. I never saw anyone buy an apple. I can visualize clearly the people in a line at least a block long at a bank, hoping to get some of their money before the bank goes out of business. Many lost everything.

One morning in 1932, my brother Barney and I were eating breakfast. We had company the night before. I must have gone to bed early because he gave me the report on the fun time everyone enjoyed. "Then came the bad news," he said. "Dad is losing his job." A predicament was imminent before which we were powerless.

Ours was the only family on our block to receive the threat from the lethal depression. Other neighbors were in established jobs which lasted.

We were new from Ireland and somewhat differently situated. Some of our differences embarrassed me. Every other mother on the block regularly hung out her laundry on Monday. My mother washed whenever she felt like it. She had no concern about conforming for the sake of conformity. I love it now.

My mother had always, always been an optimist. She trusted that if you did right, stayed close to God, and attended to duty generally, all would go well. Later that day, I saw what I had never seen before. She broke down and cried, defeated. Her lifelong outlook was shattered. There were seven children in America, bridges home burned, no land on which to grow food. What a comfort it was at that dreary moment to hear Mrs. Greer say in her Scottish burr, "We won't see you starve, Cassie" (my mother's nickname, short for Catherine). My mother became calm too. We were not alone. Those words are branded on my memory.

This is not a story of the triumph of tragedy. What fiction would not allow, reality did. The little store right across the street came up for sale, right then, with a three-story house attached. The rainy day had come but there was shelter. Dad's security job had not ended. He was asleep in preparation for the night shift when Mam saw a man observing the store and house. She got Dad out of bed. He went over, made the offer, got the store and rented the house. The other man made up his mind a half-hour later. We had ample support for the depression years and beyond. Not only was truth stranger than fiction on this occasion, but also more kind.

School, Work, Vocation

Not because of brilliance but due to my size, I was a college freshman at 16. How did it happen? When we came to America in November 1929, I at 11 was almost as tall as my brother Barney who was two years older. My mother promptly took us to the nearest Catholic school, Holy Cross in Mt. Airy. The Mother Superior was Irish and very sympathetic. She decided to keep us both together. Why she put us in the eighth grade, I don't know. We did not know American history or geography. Our teacher in Ireland was so nationalistic or unqualified that he taught us no English grammar. I did not know a verb from a noun. We were good in mathematics and spelling. I won a spelling bee but my pronunciation on the radio of "i" sounded like "a" and I was puzzled as I was hustled out of the line.

We flunked the high school entrance exam, my last failure, but the kindly nun gave us special instructions that summer, and I entered high school at age twelve. This was damaging to me. Two years difference at that age placed me in an inferior position. I related as a child to adults. Later, it was a shock to adjust to a new relationship in college.

Other considerations torpedoed my freshman year in college. I wanted to be a writer so I enrolled in Journalism. We did not yet know about left brain and right brain, but I had a theory that education dulled one's artistic sense. I was not totally convinced because I was aware that many English poets were lawyers. I worked 25 hours a week that freshman year. At 16, the social, academic, and work problems were too much. Besides, I felt I was too timid and insecure to work as a journalist. I quit college in April.

In the meantime, I had also become stage struck, though for a time that did not influence the course of life. I worked full time in a chain store until they went on strike and my mother told me to quit. I got a job in a factory on a drill press. A trained monkey, I used to think, could do my piece-work as well or better. I attended some theatre rehearsals and I noticed the qualities possessed by Tony Dwyer, an actor, and a graduate of LaSalle, my college. I could see that I needed his savoir-faire if I was going to make it in the theatre. So I decided to go back to college in April, two years exactly after quitting. I think the Lord baited me. Not long after I returned, I was knocked off the horse by the strong desire to be a priest. It was as if I were turning a clock backwards, reversing my life's course and goals. I opposed and dismissed the idea daily and it returned daily. Finally, after completing my junior year in college, I entered St. Charles Seminary to study for the priesthood. Then it took me awhile to rid myself of the feeling that my former loves, literature and theatre, were false gods.

I was in Italian language parishes exclusively after ordination and still savor the memory of that warm ambience. In 1952 I entered the United States Navy as a chaplain. That's another story.

The Holy Threesome

My brother Danny is a professor at Marquette University. I tell you that lest the comments made about him by Jean Greer and Teresa during his early years should cause you to think of him as dim witted. Children new to school are not aware of a distinction between what they have learned and what they always knew. Danny had not yet started school when he said or did something that allowed the others a startling glimpse into the abyss of his ignorance. Jean said sadly, "Gee, Danny, the Sister is going to have an awful time with you when you go to school because you don't know nothin'."

When Danny went to school his former state of ignorance was forgotten. He often played a leading role in mimicking the religious services they all now attended, Jean in the Presbyterian Church and my siblings the Catholic. Judy Boy, the cat, received the call to be the congregation. There is an American custom of blessing throats on the feast of St. Blase. Two candles are used in the blessing. Judy Boy, whose name is elsewhere explained, had his throat blessed with a knife and fork. Danny ran amok of authority when he tried to give marbles for holy communion. His penchant for twisting the moustache of authority may date from then. My mother interrupted the religious ceremony at that point. The fact that Jean and Teresa assumed clerical roles at that early date, in the early Thirties, may say something about Jungian theory. An early display of ecumenism flourished also then as contributions to the liturgy came from Catholic and Protestant sources, on one occasion as a correction. Danny was preaching. Evidently the minister at the Presbyterian Church was quite spirited. Jean interrupted Danny's homily with "You're not doing it right Danny. You're supposed to holler at them."

The Burial of Judy Boy

Judy Boy was our battleship grey cat whom Danny adored. Uncle Dan had a dog named Judy whom Danny admired, so he named the cat Judy. When informed that Judy was a girl's name, he made adjustment by calling the cat Judy Boy. Judy Boy had the distinction of being the sole member of the congregation when Danny, Jean, and Teresa conducted religious services. He duly received the blessings of every season, and, which some pastors would consider slightly heretical, he was not called on to give anything in collection. He was, however, forced to show up. The religious leaders had no qualms about female priests or a Presbyterian Catholic priest in the person of Jean Greer.

Loss of Judy Boy would have been a terrible blow to the friendly church. No congregation. But even more so, a terrible heartbreak to Danny.

One sweltering summer day, the sultry calm was shattered when someone called in our window, "Your cat is dead on the street." Sure enough, there lay the battleship grey cat. Fortunately, Danny was not home. He loved the cat so much he cried and could not sleep if it was raining and the cat was out. He would have been disillusioned if he thought Judy Boy was out chasing girl cats.

Dad was very fond of Danny, his youngest son, but very indifferent, to say the least, to his pet. Something had to be done quickly, however, before Danny got home. Dad took over and retrieved the body from the street. Our yard was part of the incline that gave Chestnut Hill its name. The ground was hard as a rock, bone dry and well trodden down. Dad got a crowbar and spade and, sweating profusely, was the main actor in the grave digging scene. Finally the hole was deep enough for interring the congregant and covering him up.

About an hour later, I went out back and there, lying peacefully on the grave, calmly pawing his face, was the illustrious Judy Boy. Of course we had to conclude that it was a case of mistaken identity. But, then, cats do have nine lives, they say. And there is the fact of all those blessings. Hmm. ...

The soulless will look beyond it all and see only Judy Boy's nighttime escapades come to light.

Geniuses of the Heart

"The heart has its reasons the mind knows not of," said Chateaubriand. Corollary to this is the thesis that the heart can discover truth which the mind alone cannot. For illustration, consider two theoretical school children. Let us suppose that, in a mathematics problem, one finds the correct answer, discovers the truth, while a second child does not. However, the teacher's mother dies. Only the second child perceives the teacher's suffering, and also realizes that an expression of sympathy by the class in the form of a card or flowers would have an assuaging effect on the teacher's grief. The first child did not perceive this truth. In reality, a child could be gifted in heart and mind, of course. But you get the point.

My brother Danny tells me that Kierkegaard had a similar idea about truth. He distinguished between what he called the genius of the mind and the genius of the will. I prefer "genius of the heart" for the latter.

There are times when my heart was inadequate and my mind knew it. I remember my mother sitting by the window, which faced the mountains, beside herself with delight as she hugged, bounced and kissed my baby sister Kathleen. She exclaimed over and over, "How could anyone not love such a little darling?" "How could anyone hurt such a precious little thing?" I was five and a half years older than Kathleen. My mind told me I should share my mother's feelings, that there was something lacking in me. However, they remained foreign to me. There was truth there that I could not perceive.

When I was 17, a baby sister died shortly after birth, a beautiful little girl. She was born at home as were all of us. The aged doctor forgot to tie the umbilical cord and the baby bled to death. My mother was inconsolable. I was very sorry for my mother. When I came home from work each day, I went up to where she was weeping in bed for days, and I tried to console her. But I didn't share her feelings for the baby, Rose Marie. My brother Barney did. I felt relieved of the disturbance and duties a baby would entail. I saw clearly that my brother's heart was better than mine which was clearly inadequate. I don't want you to come to my defense. Just give me credit for confessing.

To this day, I am amazed at my mother's attitude toward that doctor. She had no bitterness. She never ever, then or during her life, said anything like "that darned doctor." He remained her favorite. He had made a mistake. He was always kind and meant well in his care. He was also very forgetful about sending bills long before that. Or did he forget?

My brothers and sisters would agree that in our family, Barney has the perceptive heart. However, I got my idea of genius of the heart from Mabel Greer, from Bonny Scotland, Jean's mother and a second mother to all of us. Elsewhere you have read of her kindness. All one had to do was reveal a need in her presence and she responded. I remember ignobly threatening that I would say "I need that sweater" in front of Mrs. Greer. That's all it would take.

My brother-in-law Danny Gallagher was an all-heart specimen. He was one of those rare souls you could say something mean about and everyone would chuckle. His daughter remarked after he died that in all her life, he never said a mean word to her. He was related to Patrick McGill who as an author was famous in England and Ireland during the Twenties and Thirties. His books have been re-published recently. In Glenties where his picture adorns the bridge, a McGill festival is held every year. Danny was also distantly related to Peggy Noonan whose forebears were Glenties people. Glenties by the way has a 500 population.

Danny was himself a good story teller, and enjoyed without malice the fables that in one degree or other are universal. Two samples. He told of people nicknamed "The Rivers" who were, he noticed, very shy. If you were walking by their fields, from a distance you could see them busy there. But when you arrived beside the farm, they had all disappeared. Looking back you could see them busy again. They had hidden from you. However, if you took them by surprise, they were most friendly. Is there a bit of "Rivers" in you?

Another neighbor had swiftly changing moods. They could be evoked as easily as playing notes on a violin. Danny chuckled as he recounted a characteristic of the dear man who loved to have a cup of tea with the people he visited. So much so that it bordered on manic depressive. We cooked on an open fire. A chain hung down for a kettle or pot which could be hung near or far from the fire depending on whether one wanted low heat or high. Let's call him Pat. When Pat entered he was very calm and exchanged conversation in a bland, solemn manner. When the kettle was put on, he lit up like a Christmas tree and his conversation sparkled. If, by chance, someone took the kettle and hung it away up the chain, his personality slumped and he had little to say. I believe some wags did move the kettle up and down, as my mother would say, "for devilment" on Pat. There is a measure of Pat in me.

The Burial on Cape Cod

In the late Forties, the family of a friend owned two cottages near the elbow of Cape Cod. I rented them for two weeks one summer and we departed Philadelphia in two cars. My father, my sisters Kathleen and Teresa and I in one. Father O'Connor, my mother and Danny, then a teenager, in the other. Danny wasn't feeling well. He was constipated and sipped on a bottle of citrate of magnesia along the way, finishing it before our arrival at about 10 p.m. There had been miscommunication. A branch of my friend's family from New York, co-owners, were still there in both cottages. So Father O'Connor and I were bunked comfortably on Army cots in the garage. My mother, Teresa and Kathleen were given a room in one cottage. Accommodations were primitive then on Old Cape Cod. You pumped water, and used outhouses. The partitions went up just part way. Dad and Danny were consigned to the parlor floor in the other cottage. A loft where the children slept looked down on their humble resting place.

Danny slept soundly, as teenagers do, and was only semi-conscious when the laxative caused an excremental explosion without benefit of pot. The man of the house came from another room and offered to take Danny to the outhouse. Either he thought the problem was merely gaseous, or else that it was incomplete. Out they went and Danny walked into the outhouse and came right out immediately. The man said "You're quick." In a desire to correct history, years later Danny said he should have just said "Too late."

The man went back to his room. Danny now fully awake, as was dad, realized that the rug and other areas were in bad shape to say the least. Cleaning was undertaken but water was unavailable. For some reason the pump did not cooperate. Danny went out to the man's car and began wiping the dew with his T-shirt. An interesting scene in itself for the household. With the children awakened and watching from above, they wiped the floor madly and then turned the rug upside down.

Later I came on the scene and dad with his head down dejectedly said "Danny dirtied," a masterful understatement. I went to the other house to gather our group to go out for breakfast. The family staying there greeted me and conversed pleasantly with me, a strange clergyman. Danny came in and went into my mother's bedroom. Because of the half-partition we could hear his whisper, but not his words. Then my conversation about the weather and church activity was outgunned by my mother's chuckling and a loud, "Did it come on you on the hop?" an Irish expression whose meaning you can figure out and whose application you will remember. I am sure it wasn't funny then. I was embarrassed and trying desperately to carry on a dignified conversation.

The family left and then we dug a hole and buried Danny's hopelessly soiled pajamas. I am curious as to what kind of flowers now bedeck that grave.

Tact Versus Fact

As a pre-schooler my niece Joanne convicted me of being a bull in a china closet. She was sick in bed and a friend of mine, Father John O'Connor, and I went up to see her. She was a delightful child. We each gave her money and one coin was larger than the other. To test her mathematical knowledge I, left brain in operation, asked her, "Which one of those is the best?" She smiled and answered, "They're both good." I, the preacher, was preached to and humbled by a child. She realized that choosing one would be hurtful to the other person, and would lack gratitude. I am not even now so sensitive as to be aware of a double effect when I am concentrating on attaining one I have in mind. More on that later.

My nephew Bernard in an early grade in school was puzzled to see his mother hand a "greenback" to a grocer and receive several in return plus the groceries. My sister Anne explained to him the importance of the number on the bill.

There were seven children in my sister's family. Shortly after the grocery store incident, a guest gave a bill to one of them. Bernard was sitting apart on the stairs. Armed with his new-found superior knowledge, he shouted across the room to his sibling, "What number is on it?" Fellow bull, thanks for your company.

Recently, Doctor Edgar Kenton came to the rescue of us bulls. His tests which watched blood-flow images of male and female brains revealed that men when listening mostly used the left side of their brains, whereas women used both sides. The feeling-search side of Joanne's brain was also in operation while mine was dead. We can't help it if we are males, Bernard.

Penniless Jean

What happened to Jean Greer, now Jean Zeiter, should never happen to a very, very private and reserved person, but it did.

Jean grew up with our family, for many years in our house, and has been like a sister ever since. We were somewhat of a combined family with the Greers during the depression. Mr. Greer, Campbell Greer, worked at the great Stotesbury residence for which, Will Rogers said, the White House would make just a garage. They employed four hundred people to care for the house and miles of gardens. Mrs. Stotesbury wanted Mrs. Greer to take a responsible job there. In depression times, it was not wise to say no to your husband's boss. So Jean, at two, came to live with us and her parents came on their days off. After a few years, they rented a small house near us.

I used to push Jean in the baby coach. One day, Jean took to dropping her doll overboard and then asking me, "Where did the dolly go?" It happened more than once and, twice when I missed the toss, I had to back-track. At the Mass celebrating my 50th anniversary of ordination, my brother Danny, with mock solemnity, announced that I hated Presbyterians, and then related what Presbyterian Jean did to me. Jean, in a prominent seat in church, was mortified.

Jean Greer grew up to be like her mother, reserved, quite shy, non-intrusive, and, by the way, wildly generous. If someone came to visit us, the bashful Greers would quietly slip out the back door. So, again, what happened to very easily embarrassed Jean was truly catastrophic.

The old Reading Terminal in Philadelphia was busy with local trains arriving and departing in droves. It boasted the longest coffee bar I have ever seen. Jean rode there to and from her house in Chestnut Hill every working day. After work one day, she had to wait awhile for her train. She decided to have a cup of coffee. As she finished her coffee, she opened her handbag. There was no money in it. Not a cent. At that time coffee was a nickel. Sorry to date you, Jean. What to do at the fairly crowded coffee bar? She beckoned to the waitress and whispered, "I realize I have no money. I changed purses. I come here every day so I will pay you tomorrow." The decision was too much for the waitress to handle. She did not move. She bellowed her interpretation of the case, in front of everyone, to her boss at the far end of the bar. "Mabel, this woman ordered coffee and she doesn't have the nickel to pay for it."

"I come here every day. I'll bring the money tomorrow," Jean appealed to the waitress, her insensitive advocate. Jean, of course, would not ever, ever shout her defense down to the far end of the bar. Mabel, the boss, with a dismissing gesture shouted back, "Let her go." Jean quietly insisted she did not want that. She would pay tomorrow. The waitress took her cup away saying, "Next."

If it would have hidden her, Jean would gladly have crawled all the way to the train. But she had to walk off, the only entertainment there, under the gaze of uninvolved paying fellow coffee drinkers.

Dad One, Conspirators Zero

My father was a gentle, quiet man of few words. This subdued serenity was greatly furthered by my mother's volubility. He not only allowed but expected my mother to be the family spokesperson. When Kathleen was new-born, he was disturbed because my mother "trailed" after Mass and was late coming home. Trailed meant getting involved in talking to people. When she arrived, he said, "Where were you? People were coming in here to see the baby and no one here to talk to them."

His compressed vocals were at times funny without his so intending. He did have a good sense of humor but he would not guffaw or act the comedian.

My father had two attitudes which were less than prejudice but more than impatience. He couldn't stand a stupid man or an ugly woman. If a woman was good looking, stupidity did not distract from her appeal. If a man was ugly, it was no drawback, provided he was intelligent. As far as he was concerned, it was against the laws of nature for a woman to be unattractive or a man slow witted.

As my parents aged, we would more often receive news of deaths among their peers in Ireland. Dad felt obliged to send a Mass Card each time, signed by a priest, saying that Mass would be celebrated for the soul of the deceased. For Dad that meant going up five blocks to the parish, ringing the rectory bell, negotiating for the Mass card. For many, this would be a very casual activity, but Dad was a very private person, a bit reluctant to go ringing doorbells and making requests. However, my brother Danny was in the priesthood at the time and celebrated Mass every day in a Philadelphia parish. He signed and brought to Dad several Mass cards. From then on, Dad needed only to notify Danny to offer a Mass for any deceased. Dad could then fill in the deceased's name, and send the card off to Ireland. While walking out to the dining room to stow the newly received cards in the china closet, a delighted Dad was heard to say aloud to himself, "Now let them die away."

The corpses had been robbed of their power to annoy.

To Go Up
Or Not To Go Up the River

Mister Ireland, I'll call him. We used to see him in the autumn of his life, a bit bent, weary from working in landscaping, heading home. He was still a striking hulk of a man. We looked at him in awe because of the report that he had boxed champion Jack Johnson in the Army during World War I.

He had been in the same regiment with a Philadelphian wounded in the war, later a lawyer and candidate for judge. The prospective judge is well remembered because of the hullabaloo which occurred when his opponent accused him of trading on his wounds for political advantage. The criticism backfired with a vengeance.

Prohibition of alcohol was gone when we got to know Mister Ireland, but while it was in force, our man got in trouble for making moonshine. We heard that he added to his legal difficulties by throwing the plain-clothes raiders out on the street.

There were sharpers abroad in those days who intimidated the accused and solicited money, promising to fix the case. My father was similarly beset for the same problem. Just this moment, I spoke with my brother in Milwaukee who witnessed and contributed to my father's travail. In struggling to support seven children, my father brewed beer. Since people came in and out of the store, he could sell it unnoticed. The police were sympathetic and told him that he had been betrayed by a bad neighbor and they had to arrest him. Danny, then a wee boy, saw the police come inside from the store and asked them: "Do you want some beer?" A helpful son.

My father's name was Barney so I'll call Mister Ireland Barney too. He was approached by two men demanding some hundreds of dollars to fix his case. If you don't pay up, you're going up the river," they threatened. "Up the river" meant jail.

Barney refused to deal with them, took his chances and appeared in court.

When his name came up, the judge looked back and forth at Barney and the name on the docket. "Are you the Barney Ireland who served in the Army in France in the World War?" He specified the Battalion and Regiment.

"I am, your honor."

The judge left the bench, came down and shook hands with Barney.

"What a great country this would be if we had more men like Barney Ireland."

You might raise your eyebrows and question that statement, but wait on.

A lieutenant was wounded and lying exposed to enemy fire. Barney seized a machine gun and single-handedly drove Germans away. He then ran out amid the crashing shells, picked up the lieutenant on his shoulders and carried him to safety. The lieutenant was now the judge.

The case was dismissed and the judge invited Barney to lunch.

As he left the courtroom, Barney encountered the two sharpers standing by the door who witnessed the whole scene. "See," said Barney calmly, "I'm not going up the river."

Memorial Evening

In the haze of sunset's afterglow
Before a light was lit below
Looking down I saw you where
You mimicked dancer Fred Astaire

And though there was no sound at all
I heard your cheery goodby call
Joy rose, pain pierced, quick to die
Joy formed lips released a sigh.

You were so happy, so good, so young
But such to a hungry Mars are flung
And somewhere on an Eastern Isle
There came a fading of your smile.

Navy Chaplaincy

The relationship of Christians of all denominations has changed tremendously in the last fifty years. When I entered Chaplain School in Newport, Rhode Island, in 1952, Christian denominations had just about no contact with each other. Tolerance with disapproval, both in varying degrees, was the order of the day. If we thought the Holy Spirit was working in Protestant churches, the Spirit would be more than frowned on when he returned to where he belonged. Other than a retired minister a few doors from my parents, I had never spoken to a minister or rabbi. Ministers from the south in many cases had never knowingly spoken to any Catholic.

This was the setting for God to exercise his sense of humor at an ultimate level. Providence threw a host of us together, dressed as identical twins. What happened? We became friends. We recognized how much we shared in faith and values. Catholics enjoyed hospitality with lovely Protestant and Jewish families. We were the religion team. The Navy Chaplain Corps has a motto, "Cooperation without compromise." It works smoothly. Protestant chaplains evaluated me, wrote my fitness reports, and I was promoted up the line. I still receive a bundle of Christmas cards from ministers with some of whom I have been friends for forty-eight years.

A few years ago I spoke with a minister friend of my cousins in Ireland about the structure of the Chaplain Corps. He was from Northern Ireland where even tolerance is not in full flower. He found it so hard to believe that Protestants and Catholics shared offices, that one or another was the boss over a chaplain of a different denomination. It really is a phenomenal story, too little known. By the way, most of my Christmas cards come from chaplains who worked under my supervision. That would indicate I may have been a better boss than worker.

The clouds of war in Vietnam arose quickly. Service in that war zone with the Marines would be my most memorable duty. I'll take a deep breath and tell some of it. As a senior chaplain, I had it relatively easy there, but I observed many who did not.

One-Up Ray Reed

When I arrived at my first "permanent" Navy duty station, Jacksonville, Florida, I was greeted by Chaplain Ray Reed with whom I shared an office. I had just driven from Newport, Rhode Island. Snow had been falling in Newport and as I drove slowly south in an old car, the calendar seemed to be turning back to summer. It was delightful to drive in from the gate of the base on a road lined with green palm trees. I had never been south of Washington, D.C., before.

Ray's response to one phone call introduces him perfectly. He was one funny man. Someone called and asked, "What do you do with this blankety blank form number XYZ?"

"We don't use it at all."

"You have to use the blankety blank thing," said the caller, whose participles indicated that this form had a reproducing capability.

"As a chaplain I don't think I need to use it."

"Oh Christ I'm sorry," muttered the caller.

"That's a very fine act of contrition," said Ray as he hung up and nonchalantly went on to the next order of business.

As happens in the Navy, we were stationed together again in the same area, Norfolk, Virginia, and lived in the same BOQ, or Bachelor Officers Quarters. One evening a group was gathered in one of the larger rooms and several conversations were going on. My friend the psychiatrist was going back and forth with another chaplain in intense discussion about the pros and cons of immortality. Intensity led to loudness.

"Where will you go when you die?"

"The same place I came from," the psychiatrist asserted.

"How uncomfortable for your mother," said Ray Reed over his shoulder from another conversation. The balloon of intensity was burst.

A Marine Captain with control over Marine students in training in aviation technology cooperated with us, as Ray informed me, in solving problems the young might have. However, the Captain and Father Reed also needled each other at every opportunity, vying to be one-up.

The Captain sent one mixed-up Marine over for counseling one day and quickly seized on subsequent events to get the best of Father Reed. It happened that the young man tried to rape a WAVE (woman sailor) outside the theatre that same evening.

The Captain was on the phone the next morning armed with information, assuming victory. But what he didn't know was that Ray Reed had found out and knew all about the incident outside the theatre.

"Hey, what did you tell that Marine I sent over to you for counseling yesterday?" began the Captain.

"I told him to get outdoors and take up new hobbies," said Reed in a tone of complete innocence.

Only in the Navy

A few years after I joined the Navy, I was stationed at a Navy Retraining Command where court martialed Marines and Sailors served their sentences, and where a program designed to restore them to duty, better adjusted to military life, was in place. The psychiatrist in the same command and I became great friends. We lived in the same BOQ. He was super-educated, having spent twelve years at Harvard. I learned much from him and occasionally he asked for my help in dealing with a retrainee, as they were called. One evening, for example, he sought me out to ask, "What is a mortal sin?" Before Vatican II, I could be more comfortably definitive in answering.

The Navy was a completely new experience for him as it was for me, he fresh from academe and I from a Catholic rectory where I dealt exclusively with Catholic people. Our rectory, church and school were all in one building and often for days at a time I did not leave the indoors. As well as friends, we were a phenomenon to each other.

The good doctor was from the liberal wing of Reform Judaism. In my presence, he said that the Orthodox Jews were as bad as the Catholics. He was not impolite and had no intention of insulting anyone. He considered his opinions as clinical observations to which no one should take offense, academic statements that should be received as impersonal. He never ruffled my feathers in the slightest and I could also freely contradict his pronouncements. Often of course we agreed. He was an ideal choice for the type of command in which we served. True to the Jewish option for the Elohim, he had great compassion for those deprived of resources or family nurture. I was amused at his disagreement with the psychologist who considered an African American to be paranoiac. "He's not paranoiac," insisted my friend. "He's realistic."

Please wait a moment for the incident I am leading up to while I digress a little. Our country's foundational documents are based on a breakthrough made in the Jewish tradition. Even Plato and Aristotle never came close to realizing what the Jews perceived, the equality of persons and their inalienable rights. To

Plato and Aristotle they were not self-evident truths.

Back to the BOQ. The good doctor was shy. There were many women officers in the other wing of our building, but he never dated them. However, a reserve woman officer came for two weeks active duty. She was a psychiatric social worker. They had something in common so he asked her to go to dinner.

My Mass was held after the working day so when I arrived at the lounge area inside the BOQ entrance, the doctor was already there dressed for dinner in civilian clothes, pacing back and forth, smoking. He stopped me from going up to my room with "Hey what are you doing tonight? Could you come to dinner with me and my date?" He was nervous, shy and afraid the conversation would lag. I declined. As I went up the stairs (oops, ladder in the Navy) I chuckled, "Only in the Navy could it happen that the Jewish psychiatrist would ask the Catholic priest to go with him on his date."

Vietnam

To paraphrase Shakespeare, "cowards die a thousand times before their death. The valiant die but once." In Vietnam I used to ask, "Where does 365 put me on that measuring scale?" Actually, I was attached to the headquarters of the Marine Corps division, and in relatively little danger as I traveled to hold services for the troops.

Would you believe fear was not the dominant negative feeling in the war zone? Young people tend to feel immortal. Someone else is going to get hit. It takes a lot to convince young military men that death is close. However, when air support was called in and men were so close to the air targets that they could see the fins on the bomb, there was fear aplenty.

However, the loneliness of perhaps never returning home was the predominant feeling, especially in older Marines with families. The thought of arriving home in a casket and causing one's family severe grief was a constant dark companion.

Some young men were married, too. Sitting on a hillside one sunny day, a young Marine spoke in a halting way about what was on his mind. "I have a kid and wife. I don't know what is going to happen. A lot of my buddies got zapped." He had no choice. You can't quit or get a transfer. He was trapped there, as all were, for whatever fate would bring, a fate over which he had no control.

A thing rarely mentioned in reports about Vietnam is its beauty. The mountains are more individual than ridged and each is a different shade of green. Rivers emerge from them and run through rice paddies and flat plains to the sea. The beaches are gorgeous. I predicted the country would be the Japanese Riviera when peace came. That hasn't happened yet. There are birds and wildlife there galore, too. The Rabbi and I surveyed it all one Sunday morning and agreed that everything was in order except mankind.

Don't get the wrong impression of the Rabbi. He did not change the Jewish Sabbath to Sunday. We all fared better getting transportation on Sundays so he could hitch-hike with Christian chaplains and conduct what he insisted was a week-day service. So he was kosher, but I insisted he was not kosher because he had never seen the garment district in New York.

Transportation is the chaplain's biggest problem in a combat area. We have to conduct services during the week for units too small and numerous to enjoy Sunday services. Even as a Navy Commander, often I had to hitch-hike on any uncrowded jeep going my way.

The Jewish Welfare Board kept their chaplains well supplied. Over supplied. So we had many gefilte fish and matzo "parties."

Seiko watches were just $16 and $18 in those days and we equipped ourselves with them in Okinawa before the 1,500-mile jaunt to Vietnam. Numbers on the watches came up red on Sunday, one way you could tell days apart. One worked every day, morning and night, so each day seemed the same. The senior Baptist chaplain, a born comedian, said, "I know that when it comes up red, I preach."

I relieved Chaplain John J. O'Connor as 3rd Marine Division Chaplain. That was August 1965. John, later Archbishop of New York, met me at 5 a.m. in Okinawa on his way back to the "Big PX," a nickname for the United States where one could buy goods at will. He briefed me and rigged me out in Marine utilities which I had never worn before. I filled the billet of Division Chaplain for two months in Vietnam until a Navy Captain Chaplain arrived. I knew the territory which was new to him, so it was easy to be number two. We had thirty chaplains in the reinforced division. Lutheran, Catholic, Latter Day Saints, Reformed LDS, Baptists, Methodists, Christian Scientist, Jewish, Orthodox, and Episcopalian. Presbyterian came later. War brought out the best in them. To the last man, they edified me with their courage and devotion.

Contact with two Marines is an indelible part of my memory, one happy, one sad. My first day there, a chaplain with a jeep drove me around the area and pointed out the locations of several units. Before starting out, he stopped for gas. The Marine pumping the gas out of an oil drum had an Italian name on his utilities. I asked where he was from. As it turned out, Philadelphia, like myself. "Where in Philadelphia?" He mentioned an address in the area where I had served as a priest. "St. Mary of the Eternal Parish?" I asked. His eyes were wide. "Yes." He was about 19. I knew that when he was born I was the only assistant priest and baptized most of the infants. "I probably baptized you." About a month later he called to me from a truck, "My mother wrote that you baptized me when I was three weeks old." It was strange that we met so far away under such different circumstances. I hope he survived.

One Sunday afternoon the sun was shining on the green grass inside an area enclosed by a high burlap fence at Charley Med. I walked in there. There was one very young, dark haired Marine lying there. About one inch more and the bullet that entered his neck would have missed him. It killed him without messing up his hair. He was about 19, the age of my nephew. Somebody's pride and joy. His family didn't know yet that he was dead, lying alone on the green grass far from home. He was part of those who cannot testify by words in favor of some way besides war for settling human differences. But silent, he did give eloquent testimony to the waste of war.

Humor in Vietnam

Humor in Vietnam sounds like an oxymoron, but nature uses laughter to ease stress. There is always a bit of tension in a war zone at the back of one's head. Will I go home in a box or on an airplane seat? One unfortunate Marine Sergeant was in a seat on an airplane which was hit by a bullet right where he sat, killing him while his family, rejoicing, awaited his return.

Chaplains were constantly alert to ensure that their ministry decisions were not influenced by fear. So we laughed often at things that did not seem so funny later. I laughed heartily when a fellow chaplain burst out with "There I was, forty thousand feet in the air, a Coke machine and no nickel." He would have to do better now.

I wish I could picture for you one truly funny event. A Marine in muddy utilities was walking the road when the band approached from behind him on the way to the flag raising. He began acting like the leader of a parade, stepping lively, and waving to any and all on each side. The band was good for morale except when we saw them trucked off to defend the perimeter during the night. There were many jokes about what to expect from their marksmanship.

In the season before Christmas, many readings at Mass refer to the Messiah, for example, "His food will be curds and wild honey." "Curds" is not a household Marine word but "crud" is. And crud was the way it was loudly read by a devout young Marine. I was afflicted by recurring uncontrollable giggles, tempered only by the pain I was inflicting on my young friend.

The "piece de resistance" of humor in Vietnam centers on a delightful Episcopalian chaplain. He was a delicate but cheerful person, very popular with the troops and fellow chaplains. However, due to his sheltered, aristocratic background and frail physique, Palm Beach or Park Avenue would have seemed a more fitting field for his ministry.

A tidbit of Navy orientation of you serves my purpose here. When a Navy Captain or Admiral boards a ship, bells are rung and he/she announced. "Ding Dong Dong Captain United States Navy arriving."

Now for the arrival and departure of our hero. A senior chaplain who picked up our chaplain at the plane acted a bit officiously, saying at their destination, a tent in the mud, "Hop out now, act like one of the boys." The holy newcomer did not realize that there is a raised edge on a jeep floor. He hopped, tripped, and fell face down in the mud. Ding Dong Dong. Church of England arriving.

Now for his even more noteworthy departure. The night before he left, he and the Catholic chaplain had a farewell bull session in the Catholic tent, which was situated on an incline covered with lava colored gravel. The priest had dug a trench around the tent so that water coming down the incline would flow around and not into the tent. The winter monsoon is unbelievable there. Considering their denominations, it is likely that the two that night had gotten their hands on a few beers for the occasion. As Chaplain Episcopal was leaving, his host said, "Watch out for the trench." A beat too late. Church of England departing was face down in the sharp gravel, suffering slight abrasions. Next day we saw him off. His facial cuts were generously bandaged in military over-do. He was the object of many respectful looks from men in awe of this wounded hero departing so gloriously from the battle zone.

However, although the evidence of heroism was false, the heroism was real.

A Memorable Salute,
A Happy Farewell

A urinal in Vietnam consisted of a shell casing sunk in the ground at a 60-degree angle. We were solemnly instructed on accuracy in using it. Otherwise, flies of poor taste could be a health hazard, we were told.

I was using it one day when a junior officer came from behind a tent and was startled to be face to face, let us say, with a senior officer. He saluted and, of course, I had to return the salute with my right hand, in my exposed condition. Accuracy be damned.

Of sympathy, I got none from the Marines with whom I shared the story. But I found joy that no roving combat photographer recorded my activity. And when I pondered out loud about what my Bishop would think of such a picture, the Marines bent over in unmilitary fashion and howled.

However, a thief brought me joy outside that same tent a few days later. I had procured a little trunk from a Vietnamese vendor in which I stored vestments. It was partly made of sheets from which Coca-Cola cans are fashioned, as were some Vietnamese huts.

I failed to keep the trunk closed and one day I saw a rat hop out and meander out of the tent. I closed it then. I did not open it for days and when I did, I was pained to see several little dead rats. The foul stench was something else. Strangely, the vestments were OK. But the trunk stunk. I put it outside to air but with little hope of dissipating the odor. Someone promptly stole it. "My blessing be upon you," said I.

The Japanese Are Puzzled

Navy officer hats as you know are flat on top. Between this outside cover and a plastic band from front to back underneath, a business size envelope can be carried without its being bent. It was known that I used this space a lot and at my farewell dinner, the Protestant chaplain produced a hat and proceeded to pull out a foot-high pile of things.

Once at the Naval Hospital in Sasebo, Japan, I removed my hat as I approached the reception desk. The receptionist said, "Chaplain Maguire! What do you have on your head?" Seven air mail stamps were stuck on my bald spot. My quick-witted brother Danny said that I should have answered, "They're sending me home."

This was prologue only to a later performance in the Japanese countryside. This event began with an accident. A Japanese high school student, eager to catch a bus, ran across in front of my car and was knocked down. Fortunately, I was moving very slowly. He claimed that he wasn't hurt. I drove him to his country home. There I soon realized that his family were more worried about me than about their son and grandson. That partly explains why the happiest years of my life were in Japan.

I went back a few weeks later to see that all was OK, and I brought some fruit, as was customary. The first part of the journey was on a tarmac road, then a gravel road, then a dirt road, and finally, a wheel barrow path. Japanese men were working in the fields. But forget it. The sight of a shiny American car among the wheel barrows, a Naval officer in full uniform, was a sight that got all their attention.

Just the grandmother was home with half a dozen children. They walked with me back to the car. At intervals, the grandmother would burst out in thanks and I would bow and say you're welcome in Japanese.

I was conscious that all eyes from the fields were fixed on me. As I reached the car the grandmother exploded again with an unexpected expression of thanks. Again I bowed. Then I opened the car door, entered, and sat down. I was in the back seat. I could do nothing but get out as all looked on with serious faces, close the door, open the front and get in.

My brother claims that in that section of Japan, to this day, they imitate this American way of honoring their ancestors.

Blithe Spirit of the Navy

Father Sebastian Muccilli arrived in Sasebo, Japan in 1962, brand new to the Navy. As he blundered around while learning Navy and Japanese customs, I repeated many times, "It's amazing that you're still at large."

Item one: His car was coming by surface shipping and was not destined to arrive for some weeks after him. A kindly and thoughtful teacher of our congregation, Cathy Piedmont, was going on vacation. She realized that the incoming priest would need a car temporarily so she left the keys to her car for him. The first day he drove it, he rushed into my office in a flustered state.

What happened? Well, he had gone to the post office and then took the road toward the main gate. Three Marines, one on either side and one directly in front, stopped him. In his mind he reviewed what he had done. He had stopped coming from the post office before taking the main road. He had not speeded. He had done nothing wrong. So he mounted his high horse of indignation. "May I ask what is the matter?"

"Look where you are. The traffic is all backed up."

He was on the wrong side of the road. In Japan they drive on the left.

"Whose car is this?" a Marine asked. Now they were having fun because they knew Cathy, who later married their boss, Captain Fred Carr. All the humiliated clergyman could answer was "Some girl's."

We had occasion to go out the gate that evening. The embarrassed reverend was more horizontal than vertical as we passed the Marines at the gate.

A short time after, flushed and flustered again, he entered my office. "There is always a lot of shouting around a ship. Right? How can you tell who they are shouting at?" Uh-oh! What now?

There is an elaborate free standing set of stairs (ladders in the Navy) with a landing halfway up, which is used for reaching a high deck while the ship is in port. A crane hoists it aboard before the ship deploys. Our hero wanted to deliver a very insignificant report to his senior chaplain aboard. Oblivious to the ship's schedule and ignoring warning shouts, Sebastian started up the ladder. The crane operator did not see him so he swung in the dangling apparatus, waving his little sheet of paper. Finally, the ladder was put down. He delivered the paper and the ship deployed, late. Fortunately there is no war. "You might have made negative history. It's amazing. ..."

He soon topped this misadventure with another which, if it is recorded in the Guinness Book of Records, is the sole entry of its kind.

Father Muccilli is a great believer in pills and vitamins, and went to sea well supplied. Some sailors on his ship had smuggled a recently hatched duckling aboard. The duck wasn't thriving. Enter Sebastian. He ground down some pills, mixed them with liquid, and struggled to nourish the little duckling on the fantail of the ship. Suddenly, there was a call to battle stations for a surprise drill. The sailors ran, abandoning Miss Duckling. Chaplain Muccilli fitted the wee duck inside the pocket of his white uniform trousers, holding the pocket wide. The duckling, either frightened by the excitement and noise, or moved by the Muccilli pill concoction, excreted in the pocket of the white uniform.

"Today, you have made history, of a sort. Never in the history of the United States Navy has it been recorded before that a duck shit in an officer's white uniform pocket."

A cynic said, "Every man has his price," that we all, in some situation, compromise ourselves in order to feather our nest with praise or property. He could not say it about Chaplain Muccilli. He doesn't check the consequences to himself as he contemplates action. If he thinks it is right he goes ahead regardless of personal harm. As a lowly Lieutenant Junior Grade, he roused an Admiral out of bed to scold him about a family matter.

Father Muccilli remained in the Navy for nine years, including service in Vietnam in the hospital, and reached the rank of Lieutenant Commander. His personnel record was also unique. Usually marks on fitness reports are in a straight line. His zigzagged from outstanding almost to the bottom. Some Commanding Officers wanted to canonize him. Others, including the Admiral, indicated that they would have preferred to crucify him.

"Hail to thee blithe spirit."

It's amazing that you are still at large.

Two Navy Ships

The Unites States ships Capodanno and the USS Laboon are named after two Navy Chaplains with whom I served. Father Capodanno paid the utmost price for the honor. His name is on that beautiful, sad black marble wall, the Vietnam monument in Washington, D.C. He received the Congressional Medal of Honor posthumously. He was killed continuing to minister to his troops even with parts of his body shot off.

Father Capodanno had been a missionary in the Orient before entering the Navy. After Chaplain School, his first duty was again in the Far East, Vietnam. He was a tall man who reminded me of Gary Cooper. He spent two weeks with me at the Division Headquarters, getting acclimated to the nature of duty in Vietnam, and getting equipped with such luxuries as a little basin and a mirror. He taught me about looking out for oriental snakes. Then in the dark at 5 a.m. one morning I helped him embark on a helicopter for duty some sixty miles south in Chu Lai. I never saw him again.

Father "Jake" Laboon was about six feet five, a graduate of the Naval Academy where he was a star end. Army and Navy football teams were tops in the early Forties. After graduation he served as a submarine officer throughout World War II, mostly in the Pacific.

He told the story once about a time when his family was seated at dinner and watched as suddenly their car started moving out of the driveway. One of his brother's friends, it turned out, was the culprit. Years later, as often happened, his submarine picked up a downed American pilot. Even in his bedraggled state, the pilot was vaguely familiar. "Where are you from?" "Pittsburgh." "I thought so. I am Jake Laboon and you are the friend of my brother who joyrode in our car." He did not throw him back in the sea.

Father Laboon, however, was forced to jump into the sea later, forced by kindness and honor. A pilot was down too close to Japanese guns for the submarine to rescue him. Who but Jake, the top athlete aboard, could go to his rescue? They tied a rope on Lt. Laboon and let him swim out, under fire, to catch the pilot and then they pulled them both to safety. Lt. Laboon received the Silver Star for his heroism.

After the war, Lt. Laboon decided to forego what promised to be a meteoric Navy career and became a Jesuit priest. He resigned his commission. Some time after ordination, he re-entered the Navy as a chaplain. By then his classmates were Commanders, but Father Laboon was a Lieutenant Junior Grade, a rank lower than he had earned as a line officer. All his classmates knew and admired the ex-football star from the Academy. Soon they were Captains and Admirals and many wanted Father Laboon as chaplain in their command. He was a Lieutenant Commander when we were in Japan together. He had tremendous power but he refrained from ever using it except for spiritual purposes. Admirals were his friends and trusted his judgment. If he had said a ship's Captain was not doing a good job, the Captain would have been transferred. I remember a very rare occasion of a cantankerous Captain who objected to his coming aboard to conduct a service, something I never ran into. The Captain did not know him. Jake told me about the incident, and I must admit I had mixed feelings about how he dutifully, as he saw it, accepted the Captain's un-Navy behavior. He could have torpedoed the Captain's career. Father Jake was U.S. Atlantic Fleet chaplain when he retired in 1980. He died in 1988 before the USS Laboon was christened in his honor on February 20, 1993. Jakiesan, I called him in Japanese style. Goodnight Jakiesan.

Navy and Marine Corps Medal

My fifteen minutes of fame in life came in Hawaii. It was tempered by distress about other lives, but it did also involve saving life.

I had wrangled a day off during the week since I had many duties on the weekend. Relaxing in the BOQ, I started a letter to my brother saying, "It's quiet around here. Not much happens." Just then a Marine knocked loudly, opened the door and asked if he could look out the window at the military police cars arriving. He informed me that a court martialed Marine got his hands on a pistol, shot the Sergeant who got him in trouble, and was now holding a hostage in the BOQ office downstairs.

I went down. The armed man agreed to let me in. He knew me but he was enraged because I did not recognize him. The hostage sat in the middle of the room. The gunman, with pistol cocked, paced about shouting his complaints loudly and wildly. I leaned on a small safe which would at least protect my stomach from any bullets. Television programs flashed through my mind. I envied how they solved problems by the end of a half hour. I did not know how this was going to end. I talked for four hours and finally calmed the man down and he surrendered.

The Marine Corps generously recommended me for the Navy and Marine Corps Medal, their highest peacetime award, with the citation on the next page.

I have always received more praise than I deserved and less blame, which proves that people are basically generous. I hope and trust that this has been your life experience too.

THE SECRETARY OF THE NAVY

WASHINGTON

The President of the United States takes pleasure in presenting the NAVY AND MARINE CORPS MEDAL to

LIEUTENANT COMMANDER CONNELL J. MAGUIRE
CHAPLAIN CORPS
UNITED STATES NAVY

for service as set forth in the following

CITATION:

"For heroic conduct while serving at the Marine Corps Air Station, Kaneohe Bay, Oahu, Territory of Hawaii, on 23 January 1958. When a Marine, apparently gone berserk, shot an officer five times, fired several more rounds, commandeered a vehicle, and barricaded himself and the driver of the vehicle, as hostage, in a room at the Bachelor Officers' Quarters, Lieutenant Commander Maguire, apprised of the incident, immediately proceeded to the door of the barricaded room, which was surrounded by a cordon of military police. Identifying himself, he talked with the Marine for a few moments and managed to gain permission to enter the room. During the next four hours, although face to face with an armed fugitive who was at a point near hysteria, Lieutenant Commander Maguire talked gently and understandingly, gradually winning the Marine's confidence. Subsequently, the Provost Marshal and the Commanding Officer were allowed to enter the room and, shortly thereafter, the fugitive surrendered himself. Lieutenant Commander Maguire's cool courage and prompt efforts in the face of grave personal danger were vital factors in preventing further bloodshed. His conduct throughout was in keeping with the highest traditions of the United States Naval Service."

For the President,

Thomas S/aint

Secretary of the Navy

CARDINAL'S RESIDENCE
452 MADISON AVENUE
NEW YORK 22

August 22, 1958

Dear Father Maguire:

I was delighted to learn that merited recognition has been given to you and that you have been honored by receiving the Navy and Marine Corps Medal for "heroic conduct" in performance of your duty as a chaplain.

I offer you my heartfelt congratulations on the distinction that you have brought to the Chaplains Corps and to our holy religion.

With kindest regards, I am,

Very sincerely yours,

F. Cardinal Spellman
Archbishop of New York

Rev. Connell J. Maguire
Chaplain
MCAS - Navy 990
FPO San Francisco, California

Aftermath at Sawyers

Ehukai runs down to the ocean
From the mountains to the sea
In a part of Waimanalo
Sweet to me

A house on Ehukai Street
Where friendships were to start
May not be first in loveliness
It could be just my heart

Red hibiscus dance there
In winds meant to be cold
A final curtain had come down
But they had not been told.

The sea at which the house looks
Still brings glass balls ashore
By its music in the moonlight
We search for them no more

The sea casts up a lot of things
Its waves do not reclaim
Happily the sea of life
Is very much the same

Stored in my heart and memory
Are treasures time has brought
Warm and pure and heart filled hours
And lessons that were taught

Treasure trove where Ehukai
Runs down to meet the sea
In the sweetness of their meeting
Waimanalo, Hawaii

The Fall and Rise of Jack Breslin

Jack appeared on the scene at the Submarine Base, Groton, not yet eighteen years of age, full of enthusiasm for submarine life and technology. In short order, he landed in the Brig. He was caught having a beer in New London. Of sufficient years to sail the seas, he was not yet old enough to drink beer in public. His Brig sentence brought with it expulsion from the Submarine School program. Added to the shame of his being confined were his shattered dreams.

Jack's mother intervened by writing to the Commanding Officer and telling him of Jack's strong desire to serve in submarines and asking for his re-admission to the school. The Commanding Officer called Jack in. He interviewed him and finally said, "I am going to take a chance on you."

Years later Jack, now promoted to a First Class Petty Officer, had shore duty at Bethesda Naval Hospital. One day he brought papers to be signed by a patient, a Navy Captain. While going over the papers, the Captain said suddenly, "I know you. You are the guy with the mother who wrote to me. I guess I made the right decision about you."

Jack moved up the ladder. He was commissioned and eventually promoted to Lieutenant Commander. Back he came for duty at the Submarine Base, this time as the Administrative Officer. One of his duties – warden of the Brig where once he was an inmate. Talk about comeback kids!

Amens for Father Martin

The Marines, bless them, place great value on promoting cordial relations with the civilian communities adjoining their camps. On one occasion the base at Camp Lejeune was asked to provide a Navy chaplain for the funeral of a deceased retired veteran. All chaplains with the Marines, by the way, are Navy as are medical doctors, dentists, nurses and corpsmen.

The message came down to the chaplains' office as a request for a Catholic chaplain. Chaplain Martin Witting was designated to go to New Berne with the firing squad to conduct the Catholic funeral.

Going out so in the civilian community is a delicate matter for Catholic clergy. A retired person is under the spiritual jurisdiction of the local bishop and parish. It is at the least impolite to usurp the prerogative of the deceased person's pastor by entering his parish to conduct services without his concurrence. Evidently in this case, the man was an unknown in Catholic circles so a problem of protocol did not exist.

When they arrived at the designated funeral parlor, lo and behold (to coin a phrase), there was only one funeral on the schedule, two hours later than expected. The deceased and his family were not Catholics but Baptists. Miscommunication of major proportions had occurred.

What would the Protestant family feel about a Catholic priest conducting their service? The family was African American and hence predictably more ecumenical than many other Christians. The internecine battles and bitter religious controversies of European history are not part of their religious background. The family said they would welcome the Catholic chaplain and sent their thanks for his presence.

But how was Marty going to design on short notice a service that would be familiar and involve an African American Baptist congregation? In participation in worship, blacks are spontaneous and greatly uninhibited. White congregations believe in being vocally and physically unresponsive, though this is changing a little. Blacks could claim that we do not give the proper emotional response to a

-76-

truth which it deserves, that we involve only the cerebellum rather than the whole person. We are shy about letting our feelings show in public. Perhaps this is due in part to a lack of homogeneity in our culture.

Whatever, Father Marty had the problem but he thought he was off the hook when two senior Baptist ministers came to attend the funeral. But no, they would not take over because that was not the desire of the deceased and his family. At the end of the service, they would, of course, join others in saying a few words of consolation as is customary at black funerals.

So Father Martin Witting chose some hymns, prayers, and readings. He decided that the sermon he had prepared was suitable. He entered the sanctuary flanked by the two elderly Baptist ministers. As he took his seat between them and looked out on the congregation, he observed that his was the only white face in the church. When he began his homily with "My brothers and sisters in Jesus" instead of the quiet congregation he was accustomed to, looking at him stoically, there was a show-stopping "Amen brother." Throughout the sermon, it was the same, and when the people responded, Marty found himself more emotional and expressive. He got loads of "Amens." When he finished his sermon and returned to his seat between the two old ministers, one leaned over and said to him, "Who ever said you couldn't preach Baptist?"

Chaplain Witting's boss, a Lutheran, said to me later, "You can count on Marty to handle a challenging situation nicely."

Father Martin Witting was later promoted to Captain and served in the highly important position as senior chaplain at the U.S. Naval Academy.

Amen, Marty.

Dashing Aubrey

My cousin Aubrey, an Irish-English Bi-National, is not built to be a runner. He is physically stocky, and, by disposition, not inclined to rush about hurriedly. Yet he is famous in our family for a mad dash he made for the sake of decency. He may have been spurred on also by fear of the arm of the law.

Many houses in Ireland still have a small four-by-four porch in front of the main door, not for fresh-air sitting, but a place to remove mud, leave umbrellas, etc. We used to keep our milk out there long ago since that was an unheated area.

Aubrey emerged from the shower one cool day and remembered that he was to leave a note on the porch for the milkman who was due any minute. He dropped his towel and conscientiously wrote the note. As he bent over to place the bottle and note on the porch floor, the main door slammed shut and locked behind his bare behind.

Resolute and cool, very cool, Aubrey decided that the occasion called for fast, very fast, action. Only the rear of the house offered hope. So he strode out boldly, exposed, very exposed, to the elements, and ran like mad along the side of the house. In a burst of energy rarely equaled, he hammered on the window until the glass shattered. Then, in a manner less than stately but picturesque, he climbed, triumphant, within.

Unfortunately, this historic streaking is not recorded on film for posterity, but Aubrey and his neighbors preserve a clear picture of it.

The Jimmi Interview

Jimmi is a Haitian born boy. While working with sick and orphaned children in Haiti, Father Muccilli was able to help Jimmi, aged three, to recover from the trauma of his parents' death. Eventually, he brought Jimmi to the United States where he has been cared for by the Muccilli family. Jimmi has thrived in every way. Father Muccilli has adopted him and is called "Papa" by Jimmi.

Jimmi is fifteen now and attends the arts school. I consider myself a friend of Jimmi's and you will too when I tell you that I sat through thirty-five piano recitals because Jimmi was number nineteen. Two were the theme from the movie "Titanic." I didn't know it took that unfortunate ship so long to go down.

Father Seb, as he is called, helped out at C.A.P., Comprehensive AIDS Program, in West Palm Beach. C.A.P. is a place of help and consolation, of joy and sorrow. Many people come there to be tested concerning AIDS. A great number of young and old volunteers do great work there with those who are ailing and with their grieving families.

Jimmi came there occasionally after school to await his "Papa" when Jimmi was about nine years old. One day there was another person sitting there who was awaiting testing. Leaning his chin in his hand, Jimmi stared at the person in a dress, silk stockings and high heels. He spotted a five o'clock shadow and blurted out, "Are you a man or a lady?"

At the time, I wrote down the subsequent dialogue so I wouldn't forget it. I was intrigued that the man entered into a long conversation with the child and confided in him. So many people are lonely and as Dostoevski said, "People ... are more naive than we think they are. We ourselves are, too."

At Jimmi's first question, audible in the small area, Father Muccilli cringed and people at nearby desks coughed. Father Seb pondered and thought about calling Jimmi to his desk.

"I am a man, but I would like to be a lady," the man answered.

"What's your name?"

The man gave a fictitious feminine name. Jimmi didn't buy it.

"What does your mother call you?"

"John," he replied.

"Well, John, couldn't you go back to the beginning when you were a kid and find out?"

I am not sure what Jimmi meant here.

"I had a very unhappy childhood," was the reply.

"Why?" Jimmi wanted to know.

"The other boys didn't want to play with me, the games I wanted to play."

"I would play with you," sympathized Jimmi.

A thought suddenly struck Jimmi, he almost shouted and the coughs followed suit.

"You would need to find out, John, for when you go to the toilet."

This advice of Jimmi generated no response, so he summed up, "You should talk to my Papa. You are a man but you would like to be a lady. He is a priest but he would like to be a man."

No explanation of this comment was ever supplied.

The Irish Immigrant

Huge numbers of Irish immigrants came from the poor counties of Donegal and Mayo. They were easily distinguished by their accents, the lilting, muffled western accent of Mayo and the flat tones of the north in Donegal. My brother Barney's in-laws and their circle of friends were from Mayo. Barney worked most of his life for Social Security. One day he saw a man enter who had rosy cheeks and nicotine marked fingers (from smoking untipped Players cigarettes). He realized the man was fresh from Ireland and said, "Let me take this one."

We do not have Irish accents since we came here young and tried to change quickly so that the students would understand us and not tease us. The immigrant had no clue that the government representative was Irish.

"I need a Social Security KYARD."

Barney asked his name. "William Carney."

"What part of Mayo are you from?"

The man sat upright. Mayo is one of 32 Irish counties. How does this American government man know the county I am from?

"Your address?"

William gave an address of four digits in Philadelphia. "Oh, you are staying with the Matthews?"

It's incidental how my brother knew that the Matthews, friends of his in-laws from Mayo, took in boarders.

William's eyes were like soccer balls. "In a city of two million, you give an address and this government knows who is there. This American government must observe your every move," he thought with some discomfort. "In a city of two million you give an address and discover they have tracked you down already."

Finally my brother explained his Mayo connection and that he knew the Matthews took in boarders, new from Ireland. Bill pocketed his "kyard" quite relieved.

A few weeks later, Barney boarded the trolley car on his way home. Who was driving the trolley but our friend Bill Carney. He had most probably never seen a trolley until he left Ireland and here he was driving one in a big city.

Mr. Carney opened a pub and restaurant in Roslyn, a Philadelphia suburb. You can see the Carney sign there today as you drive along Easton Road. Bill is not with us any more. His remains were flown back to Mayo and interred alongside his parents.

Bill Carney was more than a successful immigrant. He is also a symbol of the benign relationship between Ireland and America, our friend in need. True, the Irish contributed much to America. Nine of Washington's generals were Irish. Commodore Barry is often referred to as the father of the American Navy. Irish Minutemen in Washington's Army are mentioned in English history as the deciding factor in the war of Independence. The lists of awards and casualties of Irish who defended America in all wars is very impressive. A disproportionate number of our Presidents were of Irish lineage. Unheralded Irish men and women worked hard, paid taxes and helped make this country great. Nevertheless, we received more than we gave.

Thanks America.

The author, at age 2½, holding puppy, in Ireland. Lady Esmond, whose husband liked to fish on the author's grandmother's property, told his mother she would "give all the money in the world" to have that darling little boy, Connell Joseph.

Johnstown Castle, Co. Wexford, Ireland

The ancestral home of Lord and Lady Esmond, who fished on my grandmother's land. Below, Grandmother's house in Glenties, the first house I remember. The photo was taken in August 1981 while driving down the Mullantiboyle Road to the driveway leading to the Gallagher farmhouse.

The street in Glenties, County Donegal, where I grew up. Below, the house that the prize turkey ran around and lost its feathers.

MY BROTHER PAT AND I
AT SPOT WHERE WE LEFT
THE CAN OF MILK
SEE "MILK CAN AFIELD"

Chaplain Maguire with two French priests visiting the aircraft carrier USS Tarawa in 1953.

Above, a photo taken from a helicopter while being taken to conduct services on a destroyer while stationed on the USS Tarawa (CVR 40). Below, returning to the Tarawa.

Above, with the sailors' choir from the USS Tarawa at Palm Sunday services in 1953. Below, with the Cardinal of Sydney, Australia at the confirmation of sailors from the Tarawa in 1954. Chaplain Maguire is at the far right.

SASEBO JAPAN | FIRST COMMUNION 1962

Above, Chaplain Maguire presiding over first communion in Sasebo, Japan, in 1962. Below, the waterfront chapel in Sasebo – the white building on the left.

MYSELF   CARDINAL SPELLMAN HELICOPTER ARRIVES FOR CHRISTMAS 1965 IN VIETNAM   CHAP DARKOWSKI

Above, Cardinal Spellman arriving in Vietnam for Christmas in 1995. Chaplain Maguire is on the left. At left, a chapel built by the engineers in Danang.

Marine Corps photo

Above, Chaplain Maguire visiting an orphanage in Danang in 1965. Left, making an all faiths charitable donation in Danang. Left to right: Chaplain Bakker, Chaplain Jones, Vietnamese clergyman, Chaplain Toland, and the author.

Above, Chaplain Maguire, second from left, during a ceremony at the Bath Iron Works in Maine. Below, with a corpsman receiving a combat decoration in 1967.

A change of command ceremony in Sasebo, Japan, in 1962. Chaplain Maguire is the officer on the right.

Above, the USS Shangri La in 1967. Right, Chaplain Maguire during his service aboard the Shangri La. Below, a helicopter assigned to the aircraft carrier.

On maneuvers at Camp Lejeune in 1977 with Baptist Chaptain Leo Stanis, who said my snoring in the tent attracted bears who thought I was one of them. Below, wearing a flak jacket, which I never received in Vietnam due to a shortage.

THE WHITE
Falcon
U. S. NAVAL STATION, KEFLAVIK INTERNATIONAL AIRPORT, ICELAND
Volume XI, No. 29   Friday, July 26, 1968

Chaplain Maguire arriving in Iceland in 1968, and being greeted by CDR R.W. Sims, executive officer of U.S. Naval Station Keflavik. In the center is CDR R.N. Klingberg.

Above and at left, the author taking part in a seder at Camp Lejeune in 1977.

The author, "in white and in step with the Marines," at his retirement ceremony at Camp Lejeune in 1978. Below, Chaplain Maguire being congratulated on his retirement by Marine General John Phillips.

Chaplain Maguire with his mother, Catherine, better known as Cassie, at age 97½, shortly before her death.

Two Lassies From Donegal

Very little was needed to frighten my mother. Yet she was exceptionally courageous in confronting formidable adversaries and serious medical operations. Perhaps there is a connection. People who are "scaredy cats" develop some immunity which enables them to cope with fear. People who have not dealt with fear can go to pieces in unexpected danger. Marines described me as "being so serene" during a tense helicopter flight whereas in reality I was scared stiff.

When, as happened often, my mother was frightened, it was hard to tell whether she was praying or cursing. She would exclaim, "Jesus, Mary, and Joseph." There wasn't time for adding "help me" which would have removed suspicion of profanity. At times it was "Jesus, Mary, and St. Anthony." I was never able to pinpoint the shade of difference in urgency which made it a St. Anthony rather than a St. Joseph area of competence.

Once in Philadelphia, there wasn't time to summon any of the above. My sister and mother had boarded the elevated train. They were standing inside as the train prepared to leave the station. The conductor made the routine call of "Watch the doors." My terrified mother, wide eyed, interpreting it as an emergency, shouted at the top of her voice, "Watch the doors!" The other riders, accustomed to occasional strange behavior on public transportation, showed little response. However, nothing can kill my sister Anne if giggles on that ride did not. Small wonder that at age 88 plus she dances every dance at her grandchildren's weddings.

Cassie, as we called my mother, had great self-confidence. Many of her peers were, in her estimation, too ready to conform to American ways. In school, we tried to overcome our Irish brogues right away and be American, but my mother's manner of speech remained unaltered. When she returned to Ireland after a 21-year absence, a friend exclaimed, "Cassie, how come you speak the same as when you left here? People come back after a year in England and we don't know a word they are saying."

"Maybe," said Cassie, "if you gave them a scare, they would talk like you again."

My mother's vintage aphorisms would fill a book. I recognize wisdom in many but some are off the wall. "Everyone has their own way of going mad," was one. With much less than substantial modification, a psychiatrist would go along with that. But "I am as far back now as the man who ate his shirt." Figure that one out.

My mother had a close friend with whom she shared adventures or transformed ordinary events into hair-raising episodes. She was Mrs. Francis Gallagher, Peggy to us. Peggy lost her husband to cancer in 1953, leaving her with five children. In 1954, she, a woman without a marketable skill other than the character to work hard, took in her deceased sister's five children, and reared them all. Patsy Dougherty, her niece, remembers the day she came to take them to her home. "She had us laughing all the way." All of them got as much education as they wished and were eminently successful. Even miracles pale before such an accomplishment.

So that is our Peggy, with us no more.

*   *   *   *

Some of us are more fervent rooters than others, whether it be for a sports team, a person, or some kind of group. Insecurity plays a part. We are comforted by the success of some entity with which we identify. But oh the pain of loss. I felt a sharper pain when the Red Sox lost than on hearing of the death of an uncle in Ireland. This, even though I knew intellectually the Red Sox loss wouldn't matter a year later, and that I would grieve for my beloved uncle forever. Interestingly, in light of what you know of my place on the family ladder, my two older brothers are not great rooters or competitors.

In 1960, we Irish Catholics were on a high as Jack Kennedy was running for President. Our self-esteem, our sense of belonging was on the line. We grew up in the ugly season after Al Smith was roundly rejected because of his Catholic faith. We had accepted as settled fact that a Catholic could never serve as the President of the United States.

Our Peggy worked by day at that time in the houses of the rich around Chestnut Hill. A Mrs. X she worked for bad-mouthed the Kennedys to Peggy. Not wishing to accept responsibility for the diatribe, Mrs. X said, "This is merely what Mrs. Y told me." Poor Mrs. Y was known as a lush. So how would Peggy choose to respond? Peggy just replied calmly, "Was she sober?" With one stroke she had turned the tables, and discredited the witness. What a lawyer Peggy would have made.

There was only one bathroom in our houses in those days. You can imagine how busy it was at Peggy's with ten children. One day, Peggy reported to do housework at a beautiful mansion. The lady of the house was going away for the day. After she left, Peggy surveyed the gorgeous bathroom with its gold fixtures, and thought why not enjoy in peace a little luxury before drudgery. Into the bathtub went Peggy. The lady forgot something, and returned to find her there. Ouch.

My mother and Peggy were forced on occasion to make emergency exits when they were overcome with giggles inappropriate to the place or occasion. Once they were kneeling in prayer at the well-known novena chapel in Germantown. An elderly priest crossed the sanctuary in front of them. Peggy whispered, "Didn't that priest get old looking?" My mother asked, "When did you see him before?" Peggy answered, "I didn't," and off they went into giggles. They had to leave for a while and reliable sources report that one of them had a personal accident due to giggle intensity.

There was an unscheduled departure from an undertaker's on another occasion. They were standing side by side at the casket. A lady came up beside my mother and said, "Hello, Mrs. Maguire. How are you? I haven't seen you in a long time." And then, "Doesn't she look nice?"

"Well thank you," said Mam.

Peggy elbowed her and said, "She's talking about the corpse."

And shortly our delinquents could be seen emerging from the funeral parlor in a non-funereal mood.

One final story is making the rounds, starring our Peggy. She catered a fancy dinner in a rich home for twelve people. As she turned to serve the shrimp, there was the cat feasting on them. She chased the cat outside, discarded the damaged fish and proceeded to serve. After dinner, as she put out the garbage she discovered the cat lying on the back steps, dead. She called in the hostess and told her, "I gave the cat a few of the shrimp and the cat died." The hostess returned to her guests. They had a conference and decided to go to Chestnut Hill Hospital and have their stomachs pumped. Some time after they had gone, there was a knock on the back door. It was the lady next door who said, "I did not want to disturb you during the dinner so I just left your cat who was killed by a car on the steps."

Curtain

Promise

At times I glimpse
My capacity for happiness

In the language of a rose
Communing with hibiscus

The glimmer of sunshine
on a slow moving stream

Rustling trees
swishing to their own music

The elusive joy
suggested by a song

The rarefied ecstasy
in an infant's smile

In moments of lightsome company
with one who penetrates my soul

Even as I dread
intensity of pain
I know
Of a heaven for me

Overdue Explosion

Friends who are of a mild, bashful disposition exist vicariously through my sister Kathleen. Things they would love to say but dare not, Kate says for them. Things and situations and even people they wish to direct to Hades are promptly consigned there courtesy of Kate. However, I played a part in a scene in which Kathleen, though exasperated, was the most restrained person on the planet that day.

Kate got all dressed up one day, white shoes, her best dress, etc. In those days there was usually one best dress for a nineteen year old in a large family. I was home on vacation from my theological studies at the seminary. I did the dishes and had to dispose of leftover gravy. Now you tell me why I put the gravy in a cup and placed the cup on the shelf with other dishes? Kate decided to have a cup of tea before leaving. She pulled down the cup. (I cringe to even tell it.) The gravy spilled all over her dress and shoes. Silently she struggled trying with white shoe polish to hide the gravy stain. I am sure she had to settle for an unsuitable dress, and wet shoes. She didn't exclaim "Why the heck did you put gravy up there? How could you be so stupid?" Not a word of reproach.

Do you know what I think? You have observed how a crying baby will momentarily go silent as they work up for a shattering yell. I think Kate must be winding up, generating an explosion which after some sixty years will be atomic.

Lecturing to Professors

One of our seminary professors was a large, expansive, self-confident priest. He was on a train trip, and in those days, priests dressed in black suit and Roman collar even while traveling. This somewhat pompous professor, or so he appeared to us, engaged the African-American porter in conversation. They discussed the weather, the trip, and eventually what work was like aboard trains, such things as the hours, salary and tips.

"I hope you don't mind me saying so," said the porter, "but the best tippers is Catholic priests and fast women." The priest understandably had no response ready. The much traveled employee then delivered the coup d'etat. He shook his head from side to side and as he moved on he added, "Easy come, easy go."

Another professor, an older priest, was very different in disposition and physique. He was shy, soft-spoken, and frail. However, beneath it all, he was ready to laugh at his own setbacks, but on this occasion at a later date only. He had relatives in Brooklyn and often visited there. He was also a Dodger rooter.

To appreciate more fully an occurrence on one of his trips from Philadelphia to Brooklyn, realize that before World War II and the Kennedy era, Catholics felt a bit alienated from mainstream America. They had been hurt by the rejection because of his faith of a Catholic candidate for President. It was axiomatic that a Catholic could never be elected President. People were of the opinion that Catholic loyalty to the Pope conflicted with loyalty to America. Al Smith, the Catholic candidate, joked after the election that he sent the Pope a telegram saying, "Unpack." During the war things changed. Young people from all denominations and parts of the country got to know, like and respect each other. No one could miss the startling number of Catholic casualties. Even from the destruction and ashes of war, Phoenixes rise.

In the former milieu we, as Catholics, were very self-conscious, anxious to make a good impression when we felt we were representing our church. We were embarrassed if even any slightly soiled laundry was washed in public. We took care that the church would not be perceived as foreign, mercenary or in any way stained. It was in this atmosphere that our little priest, anxious as all of us to uphold the honor of mother church, stood on the subway platform in Manhattan.

A black suit and Roman collar may repel some but they attract others like flies, those who have problems, or a church joke to tell, or comments they are bursting to make on life and religion.

One hulk of a man approached our wee priest and bellowed, "What are you fellows going to do for a living if the war keeps up?"

How do you answer that? Do you ask for a follow-up?

There was nothing happening on the platform to compete with this scene, so everyone turned to stare and listen. Where would the conversation go from here?

"I belong to Sacred Heart parish out the way," he shouted. "He wants a dollar every Sunday."

The on-listeners no doubt were attracted by the thickening plot but the little priest cringed and cringed some more.

A train was coming, and above the noise our man yelled, "Is this our train?"

"I said to myself," the shy priest professor told us later, "I don't care where it's going. If it's your train, it's not my train."

The Miranda Wake

The mating urge of our species and the love associated with it are strong. Tell me about them, say you. Songs, poetry, novels, entertainment of all kinds, advertising, all find in the mating game a fertile source. But there are other loves, different loves. Parents love their children and vice versa. Brothers and sisters have love for each other. For all its glorification, it is a commonplace that the feeling of mating love can fade and divorces occur. On the other hand, the love of a mother for a child has much more permanence. This lasting love is rarely sung about. Well, in Ireland, yes.

Separate from the mating love, the male and female personalities are complementary in what we might call a ying and yang manner. In "Tea for Two," the man, looking forward to children, sings of a boy for you a girl for me. Mothers have a distinct relationship with sons and fathers with daughters.

Aside from romantic love, there is a friendship love between men and women. This is not only unavoidable in society but necessary for the health and even the growth of personality. The patterns of relationship with parents and siblings can serve as models for these friendships. With a touch of cynicism, it has been said that a platonic friendship of this kind is the gun you didn't know was loaded, that it can suddenly become romantic and wrong for those bound to fidelity to another person. For the unencumbered, of course, there is no threat in all that, rather a special blessing in that they established a friendship first.

However, it remains true that there are wholesome, loving relationships between men and women that are never a threat to chastity, or conducive to wayward love. These can be tested by their resemblance to family affections. If family members are absent, it's OK. We know that they are there for us, that love abides and binds us even while apart. This love is serene whereas in romantic love, one is often racked by emotions in turmoil. As Shakespeare avers, its course "never did run smooth."

Everyone has the innate capacity to feel different kinds of love. In the childless, love for a child, a love greater than friendship, may remain untapped, never evoked by any offspring. If you agree, you will be more inclined to believe what I am going to tell you. Six years ago at age 77, I would have included myself in that percentage of you who will not believe what's coming.

There is a love in my life, a girl. "What?" you say. "You are supposed to be celibate." It's all right. I am old enough to be her grandfather. "That cuts no ice," say some of you. But I insist, she is the daughter or granddaughter I never had. She has evoked that kind of feeling. Don't you skeptics know that I would recognize a mating-type fascination, a romantic crush? I have had them. For a priest, they are a cause of tension, a disturbance of my peace of soul. They are not wholesome and sweet and bring no happiness. I don't have urgent needs to see Teresa Miranda and do so so rarely that we refer to her appearances among us as apparitions. She devotes her energy and time exclusively to the children she teaches and their families. Her day begins at 4:30 a.m.

I met Teresa six years ago when at age 77 I went with a group from Palm Beach Community College to Salamanca, Spain, for a four-week class in Spanish. We became friends, and I encouraged her to get a degree and become a teacher which she has done. I was convinced that she had so much to give to children. With a touch of hyperbole, it has been said that if Jesus were born in the twentieth century, Teresa would have been the Blessed Mother.

Believers, skeptics, and downright infidels, stay with me for the rest of my story.

Teresa's father died a few years ago. After his death, Teresa began a little story to which at first I paid little attention. As a child in Cuba, she ran out one morning as her father reached the top of the hill on his way to work, and called after him "Papi Papi." He came back down the hill. When he had descended, Teresa recalls saying, "You forgot to kiss me good-bye." Death hurts, hurts bad in such a family.

The funeral was to leave the undertaker's parlor near Miami at 9:30 a.m. on a Friday. That's about seventy heavy traffic miles from my home. So I decided I would avoid morning traffic, go down Thursday afternoon, have dinner at a nice motel, go to the wake, have a leisurely breakfast next morning and then return to the funeral parlor. You know already that this did not work out. Let me introduce two other dramatis personae, Arthur and Elena Goldfeder. Arthur is the type who calls a spade a condemned shovel, but gently.

Elena was my Spanish teacher at Palm Beach Community College. They treat me as if I am in the doddering stage and are always concerned for my well-being. I let them know my plans. I had called the funeral parlor and was informed that indeed there was a motel just across the street from their location. It had a fancy name. I gave the name to Arthur and Elena and promised to call to let them know I got there safely. I discovered later that they called the Mirandas and told them where I was planning to stay.

The motel did not live up to its fancy name. It was pre-World War II. There was no restaurant. They did not take a credit card or a check. There was a $5.00 deposit on the key. The room was dinky. There was a clean bathroom and towels, a TV bolted to the wall, and a hundred-year-old little bed. The door was an indoor type which worried me. The phone was a rotary with the center torn off. I could not make my call. I trudged over the large courtyard to the desk and was told I had to call an 800 number and charge the call. I did. Arthur answered. I said, "I have arrived safe and sound."

"You are in a whore house," were his first words. It wasn't true, I am sure, but probably unsavory characters frequented the place. Then the Mirandas called. "You must get out of there." So I never did unpack. I found an Arby's about three miles away and had a sandwich. The Mirandas insisted I stay with them. However, Cuban wakes go on and on. We might still be there if I hadn't said a closing prayer after midnight. At the crack of dawn the next day, we had to start back to the undertaker's. Of course for the wake and morning funeral I was dressed in my clericals, black suit and Roman collar. Before the service, I decided to bring the key back and get my five dollars. Teresa wanted a little relief from the sorrowful funeral parlor and said she would walk with me. She was grieving and I hesitated to come on with heavy thoughts about how it would look, a priest and a young girl handing in the key. Wow! What will my Bishop say?

Impropriety never entered Teresa's mind. To the pure, all things are pure. We walked over, I got my five dollars and my fears of the clerk's reaction proved baseless. He did not raise an eyebrow.

Perhaps he thought I was a married Episcopalian priest. If he thought so, I did not get either Church into trouble. Also, Teresa wears no makeup and has no resemblance to a woman of questionable repute. On the other hand, the clerk might have pondered over how this aged clergyman ended up with this young trophy wife. If so, my apologies to the Church of England.

Blushing in Glenties

England and Northern Ireland vacationers come to Donegal in droves. Donegal, by the way, has magnificent scenery but, in contrast to compact Kerry, its wonders are scattered. When these British tourists are dining, other than from the gentle rattle of tableware, one would barely be aware of their presence. They converse ever so softly. The English are generally deistic in religion, the Northerners actively Protestant, and this colors my scenario.

I was seated by the window, dressed in my black suit and Roman collar lest I cause my hometown relatives embarrassment by wearing more glad vacation togs. Into this quiet scene, from a door I never saw used before, bounced a man carrying a bottle of beer. He literally bounced because the step was high, at least beyond his expectations. Though it was a wide room, with several occupied tables between us, he spotted me as he sat down and shouted, "Hi, Father. Are you the local pastor here?" A layman could handle this situation better, but as a priest, I must shepherd any lamb. I explained that, no, I was born across the street and was now home from America.

"What part?"

"Philadelphia."

"I'm from Philadelphia."

"Did you go to college there?"

"Yes, LaSalle."

"I went to LaSalle."

He then gave his name, an Italian name. What he was doing in that remote corner of Ireland, I never did find out. He continued, "I didn't have the money to go there so I said to the Christian Brother, 'Do you only educate the rich? Look at the founder of your order. He reached out to poor kids.' So he gave me a break. How about a glass of this red wine? Straighten you out. You look like a movie star or something sitting over there." Twice he used the phrase "straighten you out," together with invitations to join "us" later in the lounge. My cousin, Margaret Brett, is smothered in chuckles every time that "straighten you out" is mentioned in recalling the incident.

In the meantime, not a whisper is audible from the other diners as questions and answers sail over their heads. "The Church has a lot of problems these days," said he with evident reference to news items of priest pederasty. I am sure the Irish waitresses were devastated at this public linen washing before a silent audience presumed to relish the same. Public confessions of this ilk have been anathema for Catholics and Protestants in Ireland who try to keep one-up on each other.

"Do you think priests should be allowed to marry?" As if I was about to get into that discussion, loudly, over the heads of people probably curious to know of my romantic and sexual tendencies. I ate my dinner quickly, and joined him in order to lower the pitch of rhetoric.

That was on a Wednesday. The wedding of my first cousin's daughter, Ann Edel McGill, was the following Saturday. Her cousin, Gerald Brett, who manages a fancy touristy restaurant several towns away, came to the wedding. "Did you by chance have dinner in the Highlands Hotel on Wednesday?" he asked. Did I ever! He had spoken to some English tourists at his restaurant. He had mentioned that his mother lived in the picturesque village of Glenties. "We had dinner there Wednesday evening but it was a very embarrassing experience. There was this man and this poor priest. ..."

Maggi's Creation

As a seminary student and young priest, I would not have dared to dance. Even after thirty years as a priest, this was true. The thirty years is fixed in my mind because it was in 1975, thirty years after ordination, at the Officers' Club in Groton, Connecticut, that the fifteen-year-old daughter of the Protestant chaplain, half child, half woman, not yet filling her dress, knelt down beside my table and asked, "When the orchestra starts to play, will you dance with me?" I felt like a bit of a spectacle on the floor but who could refuse so gentle a request?

Since then, I have seen priests dancing up a storm at parish celebrations. And as for kissing, my brother and I shared shock when, in the Fifties, we saw a priest kiss the bride at a wedding reception. Now cheeks are kissed all over the place. Since studying in Spain, I do both cheeks, a part of my Spanish vocabulary I do not forget.

Back to dancing. As a teenager I loved to dance and to sing, though few wanted to listen. Even now Monsignor Giliberti says that if I sing I will empty his church. I dreamed of being the next Nijinsky on the dance scene, but I never had lessons and just improvised. Though I gave up dancing to be a priest, I still had that hankering to dance. To create and be a part of beauty is not bad.

In my seventies, I joined the senior citizens in flight to Florida and found a church that welcomed my priestly help. Holy Cross, Indiantown. Some years later, Maggi Neff, doing her telemarketing to old timers, invited me to come for a complimentary dance lesson. So I went. I am still reluctant to reveal to the general public at a dance that I am a priest. I have to tell any friends, of course, so that they will know I am not an eligible bachelor. At my first couple of lessons Maggi came to the door of her office and giggled at my efforts. On more than one occasion, I said, "Get back in your office, Maggi." So I danced with a group, the oldest of which was 100 years old. I still take lessons from Philip Guinnan, a teacher's teacher, and my partner is Marian Wilson who is so graceful she would make a telephone pole look like a good dancer. Philip taught us many difficult steps. Keep in mind that none of these are what is called "huggy-wuggy," or cheek to cheek. Other than hands and arms there is no body contact. So it is graceful and modest. Recently, Philip asked us to enter a competition. We were an example of his art, his life's work. We won three first prizes and he felt proud. I wonder what you readers think of all this. My conservative origin needs reassurance that it is OK.

Maggi saw me dancing recently. Her only comment was, "What have I created?"

* * * *

EPILOGUE

Two tiny twin girls, two years old at the most, with mother in pursuit, ran in to where there was music and two dancers practicing. Within a minute, one little girl started swaying and stepping to the music. She kicked up one little foot as the dancers did. It was an incredibly sweet moment. Then she reached up her arms to her father to have him dance with her. It struck me how naturally the concept and desire of dance comes to us.

Dance has been performed everywhere and always by all peoples with both religious and secular themes. Besides beauty, it has other things to offer. For older people it is a tonic. It enhances balance and exercises the body and the memory. Try memorizing which step, which routine comes next and you will see.

People who have lost relatives and friends as they age, who perhaps now live in an empty nest, can find neighborhood friends and have fun dancing. Small wonder that elderly dancing to elderly tunes flourishes in Florida.

Maggi is not in the dance business any more, due to a tragic accident, but she could advise you for free.

Ginny

Ginny Braxton is a tall, thin, African-American woman. A lot of people are. But there is only one Ginny. Ask her mellow husband or the super children they spawned. Ask anyone who knows her. She has been a newspaper columnist, and has written a musical play and a book of poems. She wrote a memorable poem as she surveyed the empty downstairs in my house the day my mother died. Her energetic kindness is endless. Right now she is teaching in order to give back some of what she received.

I met Ginny when Joe DeMarco and I were forming a writers' group which was to meet in downtown Philadelphia. I lived in Chestnut Hill with my mother. Joe called and said there was a girl, as he put it, who wanted to join the group, who lived near me and had a transportation problem. She could ride with me, Joe said, but "she's afraid to come to your area because she is black." What a way for a person to go through life, always on edge lest you be rejected or hurt by some form of scorn! Such a threat would make me reclusive and hostile, but blacks are forgiving. How unaware I was of this suffering right before my eyes on all sides, a pain that is still inflicted all around us.

I responded to Joe, "Tell her that if she comes near here, I will beat her up." Five minutes later, I got a call in a lilting voice, "Where do I come to get beat up?"

My mother called Ginny "the wee girl from Wyndmoor." Ginny wrote in her column that when Mam said that about her, she felt as though she had inherited the crown jewels. However, my mother had a cataract operation by Dr. Brown which restored her sight to a miraculous degree at age 94. But with the miracle, Ginny's crown jewels went down the drain. The next time my mother saw Ginny she said, "Huh. She's not so wee at all." My mother did not ask again, "Did your people come from Ireland?" To which Ginny used to reply with a smile, "I don't think so, Cassie."

Ginny was the lector for a scripture reading at my fortieth, forty-fifth and fiftieth anniversaries of my ordination to the priesthood. At my fiftieth, my nephew, Tommy, recited the Our Father in Gaelic. Before Mass, I mentioned that

Ginny's ancestors in northern Africa knew the Our Father long before St. Patrick taught it to the Irish. But I pointed out that they did not know it in Gaelic, and if any of them did, their accents were awful.

Shortly before she died, Ginny's mother wrote a beautiful farewell letter, a form of will to her children. She, too, was a tall, thin gracious lady. In physique and character, Ginny did not come out of the ground. I am glad I met the mother before she became disabled.

I called Ginny and told her I was writing this book and wanted a copy of her mother's goodbye letter. Ginny said, "Be sure you include in your book the story of the two blackguards," one of many Irish stories I told while chauffeuring.

Blackguard is pronounced BLAGGARD and in Ireland and England was synonymous with our word scoundrel. The word, no doubt, had its origin in some unpopular military or law enforcing outfit which wore black uniforms. The story was about my two brothers escorting a boy from a neighboring farm to his first day at school. He cried all day. At recess time, he was jumping up and down in tearful frustration and misery. However, even on the way home, he displayed no ill will toward my brothers, not until he reached their lane and they left him. He knew he was safely near home then and safe from them as he threw stones after them shouting, "Go home you blaggards."

While Ginny was still searching for the letter, I found a copy in my own files. I called Ginny and got the answering machine. I left the message, "I found what I needed, so you can go home, you blaggard."

Here are the words of Ginny's mother before she died.

"I do not wish any great display of tears or mourning. I am quite glad to give up this world and this life. I love my children and am very proud of the way they have grown up. As I failed in keeping them a father and was therefore more a provider than a mother, I felt the one thing I could do was to free them of any obligation to me. And so I've done my best to not cling or demand. They may think I don't deeply love them, but this has been the hardest, lonesomest thing I've done in all my experiences. A little piece of me died every time one married or moved and especially when they left Philadelphia. Their successes have been my crowning glory in this life. All I can really bequeath them is the sincere knowledge that their lives have pleased me and made my life full of sunshine. Because you all are lovely people, I've seen and done so many wonderful things that couldn't have happened had I not had you. I've learned some lessons, gained some needed knowledge and seen the reasons for what might be considered my failures by watching you all advance. And so you all were well worth any struggle I had 'cause I was happy when I was doing it though I didn't know how much until you all left. You've brought me nothing but joy and fun for which I most sincerely thank you.

"Now I also pray that your children will bring you joy, fun, love and glory on this Plane. But do know that my one desire for each of you is still that you reach out and get Love, God, Jesus or the Christ Spirit within you and your lives. Give Him the first Honor. Seek His Will first in All things and teach your children so to do and your life will be even better than mine. For the greatest happiness is being close to the Spirit knowing He knows you so well that you see and feel His Will in everything you do and have that Peace that lets you know no one can harm you.

"I am to try to advance and be more of a success in Spirit than I was in body but I'll always be close enough to know what is going on and help smooth out the rough places if I ever see you need that kind of help.

Love, Hugs

XX XX XX

Mom"

Indeed Ginny did not come out of the ground.

Sheila

Twenty-some years ago, Sheila Cohen said I should write novel-type prose instead of plays and poetry. Sheila, who managed the building, and her son Henry, an actor, lived right across the hall from me and my invalid mother. She and another lady, Pauline Bernstein, made sure that the first fruits of their culinary skills were sampled by my mother.

Sheila had cancer which soon killed her. But, oh, how the memory of her sense of humor lives on. Equal rights for women were a hot topic at the time. One night it happened that three women took my place caring for my mother, due to something such as time restraints, cooking skill or lack thereof. Next day, as Sheila was heading down the corridor toward the elevator, I called after her, "It took three women to take my place last night. And you think you are equal?" She did not turn around or respond but I could see her shoulders shaking with laughter. A few days before she died, totally bed-ridden, and, I am sure hurting physically and emotionally, I told her about what I described as our new system. It had happened that my sister Kathleen told me of a birthday card she saw and wanted to buy for me, but for some reason she didn't. I told Sheila that the way we do it any more to save time, trouble, and money is to tell each other, "Your birthday greeting card is the fifth one in, on the third row from the bottom. Go look at it and enjoy." The covers on her death bed shook with laughter.

The Cohen family asked me, a Catholic priest, to give the eulogy at Sheila's funeral. The Rabbi graciously consented. I have lost that sermon in which I commended her to the God of Abraham, Isaac, and Jacob, Sheila's God.

In this book I have taken your advice Sheila. Bless my efforts. But allow me to add a little skit that was scened in the lobby of the building you managed. It has nothing to do with your life but I named the lady Sheila.

Sunset in the Lobby

By

CONNELL J. MAGUIRE

TIME

The present

PLACE

A large suburban apartment house lobby

CHARACTERS

Richard Jordan, 86

Sheila Jordan, 82

Richard and Sheila Jordan are seated facing downstage at a slight angle. His chair (later hers) is a rocker.

Sheila

Richard, this chair is not where it used to be.

Richard

So, what's wrong with that?

Sheila

I can't see who's getting on and off the elevator.

Richard

Can't you move your chair?

Sheila

How could I do that? It's too heavy.

Richard

Sit over here.

(They exchange places slowly)

I don't know who you expect to see anyway. You can see the sunset better from here. It's beautiful.

Sheila

I like to look at people.

Richard

The sky is one big glow in the west.

Sheila

I wonder who she is.

Richard

She's the new secretary.

Sheila

Leave it to you to know.

Richard

When you pay the rent, you see her.

Sheila

Is she Jewish?

Richard

I don't know.

Sheila

What's her name?

Richard

She can hear every word you're saying.

Sheila

What's wrong with that?

Richard

You shouldn't be talking out loud about her.

Sheila

I'm not saying anything out of the way. Did I say anything wrong?

Richard

Good morning, Miss.

Voice off

Good morning, Richard. Is that Mrs. Jordan?

Richard

Yes. My wife, Sheila, Mrs. Richard Jordan the First

Voice off

How are you, Mrs. Jordan? Nice to see you both.

Richard

My wife was asking about you.

Sheila

I didn't say anything out of the way.

Voice

My name is Jean Morasco.

Sheila

Is that Jewish?

Voice

No. It's Italian.

Richard

Same thing. I mean it makes no difference.

Voice

Have a nice day.

Richard

Same to you.

Sheila

Where is she going?

Richard

Back to the office. She picked up the mail. Couldn't you see? Boy. She's a looker.

Sheila

What a thing to say!

Richard

Can't I say she's a looker?

Sheila

Not with so much oomph.

Richard

What oomph! Where am I going to get oomph at 86 years of age?

Sheila

I'm glad you're 86.

Richard

Instead of 90?

Sheila

You always had an eye for the pretty girls.

Richard

Nothing wrong with that. I had an eye for you, didn't I?

Sheila

I looked just as good as she does, in my day.

Richard

Better.

> He catches her hand. He doesn't let go
> for the rest of the play.

Sheila

Richard. Don't be holding my hand here.

Richard

Why not?

Sheila

It's not the place for it. What will people think?

Richard

What will they think? We're married, aren't we? We've been married for sixty years.

Sheila

All kinds of people walk through this lobby. They don't know.

Richard

You want me to go upstairs and get our marriage certificate, and hold it up with the other hand?

Sheila

You're always doing something silly.

Richard

When do I do something silly?

Sheila

When? From day one. That's when. On our honeymoon in Hawaii. At the King of Hawaii Hotel.

Richard

It was the Royal Hawaiian.

Sheila

You in that fancy lobby with that skirt on you.

Richard

That's no skirt. It's lava lava.

Sheila

(Smiles) Naked from the waist up. Dancing one of them hulas and singing up to me on the balcony. I got away from the railing as fast as my feet would carry me.

Richard

You laughed yourself sick all night.

(They smile silently for five seconds)

Richard

I should have kept the lava lava. Put it on and come down here. Do a hula the day they're all down here waiting for their Social Security checks.

Sheila

You'd give some of them a heart attack.

Richard

Somebody should put a little life in this place.

Sheila

If the cops didn't lock you up, the psychiatrist would.

Richard

We should go back to Hawaii for a visit.

Sheila

You and me!!! Nonsense.

Richard

Why not? See the old place. Walk around all the places where we walked back then. Look out at the same beach.

Sheila

How could we ever do that?

Richard

Just get on a plane and away we go.

Sheila

What if you got sick out there?

Richard

That nice weather might do me good.

Sheila

Nonsense. (Giggles) One thing I know. If you did one of those hulas now, you'd break your back in two.

Richard

That was a great time, wasn't it? The bright sun on the blue water. I can see it. You always laughing in the surf. You looked like a movie star. Only natural. Like a farmer's daughter.

Sheila

Like a farmer's daughter? I'm a city girl.

Richard

I mean you looked natural. You had pink cheeks. Blue eyes. You didn't need make-up. All the fellows used to look at you. I wondered if I could hold on to you. It's a wonder it didn't kill me, loving you so much.

Sheila

Hush up that silly nonsense. The doorman can hear you.

Richard

Oh, you like it. Silly nonsense or not.

Sheila

Have sense. We have thirty great-grandchildren.

Richard

So we have sixty, a hundred great-grandchildren. We had great days. I don't care who knows it. Great days back then.

Sheila

You and your old memories. What's the matter with today? This is as good a day as we ever had. We started off with a nice breakfast together. I fixed your eggs just the way you always liked them. Over easy. And you ate them all. We had lunch. And when you're finished with your sunset, we'll have dinner. Watch TV. What's the matter with all that?

Richard

Where did you get those pretty big, blue eyes?

Sheila

Oh, hush up.

Richard slumps over to one side of his chair, face down, letting go of her hand.

Sheila

Richard. (She puts her hand on his shoulder) Richard. Oh my God. Oh my God. Doorman. Please. Call 911 (she leans over on Richard). Oh Richard, Richard. Take me with you.

Blackout

* * * *

Goodnight Sheila

The Story of Life

Who would not through fragrant fields
Sampling the nectar springtime yields
Forever stroll, to ever know
Enchantment where the daisies grow

But poignantly a theme will play
And sound us out for harmony
Moments passed in flowers are
Whispers from a waiting star

We may not just in springside live
A call for purpose bids us give
Firm loves are fair, but blossoms must
Engender fruit or turn to dust

A Dancing Man

By

CONNELL J. MAGUIRE

A Psychiatrist's Office
in a Hospital for the Emotionally Disturbed

Characters

Jerry Sands	A patient
Sharon Helfern	Out-patient
John Helfern	Her husband
Dr. Kraus	A Psychiatrist

TIME

PRESENT

A DANCING MAN

Stage left is a psychiatrist's office.
There is a window on the left. The
furniture consists of a desk, a few chairs
and a closet containing white coats. A
few diplomas hang on upstage wall.
Stage right a corridor runs up and down
with an entrance to the office. Box of
tissues with one sticking up on desk.
Jerry enters by the window, tiptoes over
and locks the door. He sits, puts his
muddy feet up on the desk, and dials the
phone.

JERRY

Hi Mam. ... It's OK. Nobody here but me. My garden is right outside. Listen
Mam. On Thursday could you bring me some seeds and bulbs? **(Looks at shoes.)**
And a brush to get the mud off these shoes. ... Oh yeah Mam. Dr. Kraus is nice.
My dog Trixie is the only one who treats me better. Yes. You too, Mam. But
Trixie never scolds me. He never gets mad at me. Always forgives me.

(John and Sharon enter and come
downstage toward office door. John is
smoking a cigar.)

JERRY

OK. See you on visiting day Mam, Thursday.

JOHN

Here it is. **(Jerry stops to listen.)**

-114-

SHARON

Oh my God, yes.

JOHN

Dr. A.J. Kraus (Looks at his watch.) We're early.

JERRY

I better run now, Mam. Goodbye.

(Jerry hangs up and tiptoes over to door
and listens.)

SHARON

I hope he's a good psychiatrist.

JOHN

I hear he's a very good psychiatrist. The best.

SHARON

I sure hope so. I'd hate to go through all this agony with some quack.

JOHN

I'll size him up myself as soon as we get in there. Just like that **(snaps his
fingers)**. Nobody pulls the wool over my eyes.

SHARON

I'm so glad I don't have to come again.

JOHN

I wish you would.

SHARON

Don't start that. I agreed to come to one session and one session only.

JOHN

We never have a happy day anymore. You're always in pain. You really need
help.

SHARON

Would you want someone accusing your dead mother of making you sick?
That is what he will do.

JOHN

He may not do that at all.

SHARON

He'll do it. They all do.

JOHN

Maybe he'll just give you a prescription.

SHARON

No he won't. Wait and see.

JOHN

When I went to the shrink that time, he didn't badmouth my mother.

SHARON

You weren't depressed.

JOHN

I wasn't depressed? After my boss wrote in my record that I was immature, and who the hell ever hired me. I wasn't depressed.

SHARON

That's different.

JOHN

It was a lot worse. That's how it's different. I'm as mature as anyone on the force.

SHARON

Did the doctor say that?

JOHN

He hinted at it. I can take a hint. That's part of being mature.

> (Jerry laughs. He starts to clean muddy shoes and desk with tissues but they are not thick enough. He throws them out the window. He takes out his handkerchief, tries that on shoes and then winds up cartwheel style and throws

the handkerchief out the window.)

SHARON

Let's wait inside.

JOHN

"Doctor is out," it says.

SHARON

There is someone in there. Let's go in. Get it over with.

JOHN

OK.

(Sharon catches his arm as he reaches for the knob.)

SHARON

Now remember. Don't let me down in there.

JOHN

What do you mean?

SHARON

Don't tell him I'm depressed.

JOHN

But that's crazy. How can he help you if you don't tell him?

SHARON

OK. Let's call the whole thing off. I'm not going in there.

JOHN

But, darling, you can't sleep at night. You feel miserable all day.

SHARON

Coming here is the worst misery.

JOHN

Well tell me what you want me to say and I'll say it.

SHARON

Just tell him that I worry a lot. That I used to be depressed but I'm all right now.

JOHN

OK. I'll do just that. But you must keep your share of the bargain.

SHARON

What share?

JOHN

No matter what happens, don't change your mind in there and try to run out.

SHARON

Once I'm in there, I'll grin and bear it.

JOHN

OK. **(Tries door.)** The door is locked. **(John knocks.)**

JERRY

Who's there?

JOHN

We have a 2 o'clock appointment with Dr. Kraus. John and Sharon Helfern. We are ten minutes early.

JERRY

Oh yes. Of course. Just a minute please.

> (Jerry goes to the closet and takes out a white coat. He puts it on and looks it over. It is too long.)

JOHN

I talked to you on the phone. I told you. ... I mean I made an appointment for my wife.

> (Jerry opens the door and makes a sweeping gesture.)

JERRY

Come right in. Have a seat.

> (They sit.)

JOHN

Do you mind my cigar, Doctor?

JERRY

No. Give me a puff.

> (John gives him the cigar and Jerry takes a puff. He coughs wildly and hands cigar back.)

JOHN

They're for a very mature man only, Doctor. Hah.

JERRY

I guess so. **(To Sharon.)** Do you have a handkerchief?

SHARON

(As she hands it over.) I hope it isn't soiled.

JERRY

It's perfect.

> (Jerry puts his foot up on a chair and wipes his shoes with the handkerchief.)

In the garden you pick up so much mud. Tissues just don't do the job. I even got some on the desk.

> (Wipes desk. He winds up as before and pitches the handkerchief out the window. As he does so he chatters and turns to

"first base" before throwing.)

JERRY

Doctor Jerry eyes the runner at first. Gets the signal and zing. Strike!

(He models coat.)

How do you like me in this?

JOHN

Looks just fine, Doctor.

JERRY

It's a little long I think. Do they wear them this long?

JOHN

My wife would be a better judge of that. She is a dressmaker.

JERRY

What do you think?

(He walks up and down.)

SHARON

It is a little long.

JERRY

You could take it up. As part of the fee.

JOHN

Sure she could.

JERRY

OK.

SHARON

All right, Doctor.

JERRY

Good. Now what. **(Sits at desk.)**

JOHN

My wife used to be. … You tell him, Sharon.

SHARON

First of all, we don't want any more appointments.

JERRY

That's too bad.

JOHN

That's what I say.

JERRY

I need the money.

JOHN

We will be glad to pay for this one of course.

JERRY

(Puts hand out.) OK. Put it there.

JOHN

Now?

JERRY

Sure now. Somebody might come in.

JOHN

(As he takes out checkbook.) It says "Doctor is out" on the door.

JERRY

It does? I must check out there.

> (Opens the door and looks up and down the corridor.)

I don't hear a thing, do you?

JOHN

No.

> (Jerry tiptoes up the corridor and looks around corner)

SHARON

He is strange.

JOHN

Relax. He's what they call eccentric. He's OK.

SHARON

OK? John, he's weird.

JOHN

Now there you go.

SHARON

There I go where?

JOHN

Looking for an excuse not to cooperate. Even this one time.

SHARON

I'm not. Don't you notice him strange? My God.

JOHN

That's how they are. They're all a little funny. They get like their patients.

SHARON

I'm a patient and I'm not like that.

JOHN

Keep your side of the bargain. I am keeping mine. In this business, it's perfectly normal for them to be a little. ... **(Gestures to indicate nuttiness.)**

SHARON

He is more than a little.

JOHN

Now listen. We didn't come here for you to diagnose him.

SHARON

Somebody should diagnose you and him both.

(Jerry returns to office.)

JERRY

I'll just bolt this door.

JOHN

(Still holding checkbook.) What is your fee, Doctor?

JERRY

Seven dollars and eighty-three cents.

JOHN

$7.83? That's very reasonable.

JERRY

But this is such fun. Forget the money for now. Isn't this fun? **(Sits at desk.)**

JOHN

Well, it's serious for us.

JERRY

Why?

JOHN

My wife used to have anxiety and depression.

SHARON

I'm only a little worried now.

JOHN

She's OK now.

JERRY

That's why she came to see the doctor? Because she's OK?

JOHN

Yes.

JERRY

Did you go to the doctor before when you were depressed?

JOHN

No, this is the first time.

JERRY

Hah! When you are depressed you don't go near the doctor but when you are OK you do. Hah. Hah. You two are strange. You're my kind of people. Hah, hah.

JOHN

Well, it's a long. ...

SHARON

I just got OK recently.

JERRY

No problem. Listen. If it wasn't for strange people like you, this building wouldn't be here. Where would psychiatrists be today? Ever think of that?

JOHN

There's a lot of truth in that.

JERRY

Thank God for nutty people I say. Right?

JOHN

Nutty doesn't describe me exactly.

JERRY

What do you do while she is dressmaking?

JOHN

I am a police officer.

JERRY

I didn't do it. I am not a robber.

> (Jerry ducks his head under desk. John ducks his head under other side of desk.)

JOHN

Hah. I don't chase robbers normally. I patrol the highway.

> (They both sit upright.)

JERRY

I have a friend who is a robber.

JOHN

Oh?

JERRY

He steals from the hospital store.

JOHN

Is he a doctor?

JERRY

I call him a fellow practitioner, small words and curses are a big no-no around here.

SHARON

I am afraid we are wasting your time and ours, Doctor.

JERRY

Time? Who cares about time? So, you did have a bad problem?

SHARON

Yes. I just felt down, Doctor.

JERRY

Does he treat you like a dog?

SHARON

Certainly not. He has nothing to do with it.

JOHN

Wait a second, Doc.

JERRY

(To John) You don't treat her like a dog?

JOHN

Of course I don't. I'm no problem to her at all.

JERRY

If you don't treat her like a dog, you're a problem.

JOHN

I treat my wife like a lady.

JERRY

That's too bad.

SHARON

I've heard everything now.

JOHN

Even I don't understand you now, Doctor.

JERRY

Did you ever have a dog?

JOHN

Sure.

JERRY

A dog always licks you and loves you, even after you beat him or scold him. Or leave him all alone shut up. He forgets and forgives and jumps all over you.

(Jerry pants like a dog.)

JOHN

Yeah. I know all that.

SHARON

John, he means you should love me and forgive me and all that stuff, act like a dog does. Do you see?

JOHN

Oh! I see now. Hey. You do make sense. In a funny sort of way. People should be more like dogs, right? That's great.

JERRY

My dog Trixie is the best person I know.

JOHN

See what I mean, dear? Underneath it all, he makes a lot of sense.

JERRY

Underneath all what?

JOHN

I explained to my wife that you all are what they call eccentric.

JERRY

That's not the word on my chart. **(He illustrates.)** It's a big, long word.

SHARON

This is all nonsense to me.

JOHN

Why?

SHARON

Why? I don't want a dog for a husband, that's why.

JOHN

Why not?

SHARON

Why not? Do you hear what you are saying? Do you? Did I get married to have a barking animal snapping at my heels?

JOHN

Dogs only do that to strangers.

SHARON

Listen to yourself. This whole conversation, this whole scene is crazy.

JOHN

No it's not.

SHARON

You're not my problem. Not this one anyway.

JERRY

This one? What do you mean "this one"?

SHARON

My depression. The depression I used to have.

JERRY

What is he then? There is a word –

SHARON

He is supportive.

JERRY

Yeah. That's it. Page 22 in that doctor's book.

JOHN

(Pats Sharon's hand.) Thank you, dear.

JERRY

(Smiles.) What things do you like about him?

SHARON

Oh, lots. … Some I don't.

JOHN

Mostly she likes my maturity, I'd say.

JERRY

What's that?

JOHN

What's that!

JERRY

Yeah. What's that?

JOHN

Oh, you want me to say. OK. It's being "with it." Knowing where it's at. No flies on you. That kind of thing. Nobody's fool. Having it all together. Your head on straight.

JERRY

All that?

JOHN

Yeah. That makes her feel secure.

JERRY

I see. **(He rises.)** Do you dance with her?

JOHN

No. **(Jerry starts to dance.)** We like to listen to music.

JERRY

Why not dance to it?

JOHN

I am just not a dancing man.

JERRY

I am.

> (Then he half-sings four times "I am a dancing man," kickout at "am" and "man." The kicks come close to Sharon and John and they move their chairs back a little. The phone rings. Jerry answers.)

Yes this is the doctor. What's a doctor supposed to do about ants on your table? Don't you have a husband? Oh, he's one of the ants. Hee. Hee. Well, my Mama always says if you can't beat them, eat them. ... Right. Pour chocolate syrup on them. I didn't say you were a cannibal. **(Puts receiver down.)** She hung up. You just can't have a normal conversation with some people.

SHARON

That's coming through loud and clear.

JERRY

Where were we? Oh yes. Your husband is a supporter rather than a problem.

SHARON

The whole thing has nothing to do with my husband at all. Nothing. He didn't cause my problem.

JERRY

Who did?

SHARON

I don't know who. Or what.

JERRY

Oh yes you do. You know he didn't because you know who did. You're hiding something.

SHARON

I am not.

JERRY

Oh yes you are. She has an idea and she is hiding it. I can tell.

SHARON

I do not.

JERRY

She's hiding it like cookies and candy and she won't tell us. She wants us to guess. She does. She does.

SHARON

You can guess all you want for all I care.

JERRY

OK, John. Let's start, is it animal, mineral, or vegetable?

JOHN

I thought it was cookies and candy.

SHARON

This is sheer nonsense. Honest to God, I never. ...

JOHN

Well, you should tell him something. Give him something to work with. You see, Sharon doesn't want to talk to you.

SHARON

Psychiatrists make you say bad things about your mother.

JOHN

She means you would blame her mother for her depression.

JERRY

Me? If she doesn't blame her, I won't blame her. Not old Jerry. Not Doctor Jerry. I love the sound of that. Dr. Jerry.

SHARON

I want my mother to rest in peace.

JERRY

So do I.

JOHN

But she could still talk about their problems, couldn't she, Doctor?

JERRY

To psychiatrists? They might lock her up. So your poor mother died?

SHARON

Yes. Two years ago.

JERRY

You loved her a lot?

SHARON

Yes.

> (She wipes a tear. She has to get tissue
> from desk to do so. She takes about
> three.)

JERRY

My mother is living. She has a flower garden. Did your mother have a flower garden?

SHARON

As a matter of fact, she did.

JERRY

She did? What did she plant?

SHARON

Oh, roses, seasonal flowers. She had azaleas. Some vegetables.

JERRY

Were you scared of your mother?

SHARON

Yes.

JERRY

I was scared of my mother. Still am.

SHARON

I couldn't talk to my mother.

JOHN

You never told me that dear.

SHARON

I loved her but I was afraid of her.

JERRY

So that's it. That's it.

SHARON

That's what?

JERRY

The thing you were hiding.

SHARON

What do you mean?

JERRY

You think your mother is the one to blame. She made you depressed.

SHARON

(Angrily.) I do not. I do nothing of the kind.

JERRY

Didn't she give away what she is hiding?

JOHN

Not exactly.

JERRY

You think so. You think that it's your mother's fault that you're mixed up.

SHARON

(Rises and almost screaming.) No. You see what I mean? He is trying to put words in my mouth.

JOHN

Easy dear. He's really only asking you.

SHARON

(Cries.) I told you it would be like this.

JOHN

Easy dear, we won't come back after today.

SHARON

I want to go now, John.

JERRY

You are a strange one, you are.

SHARON

Because I respect my mother's memory? If that makes me strange. ...

JERRY

Because you blame your mother.

SHARON

I don't blame my mother. You do. I knew you would.

JERRY

You are all wrong. You are absolutely wrong. You are all mixed up.

SHARON

I am not wrong. I am not mixed up. Let's go John.

JOHN

Easy dear. Listen to the Doctor. Sit down. Please. The Doctor may have a point.

SHARON

His point is that he condemns my mother. Didn't you hear him?

JOHN

(To Jerry.) Did you say her mother was to blame?

SHARON

He wants me to say it. He wants me to think my mother made me depressed.

JOHN

Be calm for a minute, dear. Let's straighten this out.

SHARON

(Sits.) I told you it would be like this. Oh, God.

JERRY

I know how to explain it all and make Sharon happy. I have a great idea.

JOHN

You do?

JERRY

She is no farmer that woman you married.

JOHN

No. … We live in center city.

JERRY

They don't have ducks and chickens down there, do they?

JOHN

No. Just dogs and cats and things like that. They have pigeons of course.

JERRY

Do they know a duck from a chicken down there?

JOHN

You must be kidding.

JERRY

How do they know?

JOHN

Everybody knows that.

JERRY

How?

JOHN

From ads, movies, TV and things like that. Trips to the country.

JERRY

Tell you what then. I am a chicken **(Starts to climb on desk)** and you two will be ducks. Wait a minute.

> (Comes down from desk, goes into closet and closes the door.)

SHARON

(She gets tissue and wipes tears.) He destroyed my good handkerchief. Did you see where he went? Into the closet.

JOHN

That's another room.

SHARON

(Sighs.) It's not another room. It's a closet.

JOHN

Well. He'll come out again.

SHARON

The point is not that he will come out again. The point is he went into a closet and closed the door. I can't believe this.

JOHN

Well, he thinks we act strange, too.

SHARON

He needs a doctor more than I do.

JOHN

He's not in pain like you dear. He's happy.

SHARON

Let's get out of here.

JOHN

No. No. Wait.

SHARON

I'm more upset now than when I came. Let's go.

JOHN

We have to pay him.

SHARON

We can mail it to him.

> (She rises. John rises. Jerry starts out. He is wearing and examining a shorter coat.)

JERRY

(Hands Sharon folded up coat.) This is much better don't you think?

JOHN

Looks fine, Doctor.

JERRY

(Gets up on desk.) This is going to be so exciting. I am a chicken, a mother hen. And I have a problem. They put two duck eggs under me and I hatched two ducklings instead of two chickens. You are two ducklings.

SHARON

First we're dogs. Now we're ducks.

JOHN

But this doesn't hurt you. **(John grins.)** This is fun.

JERRY

This is not funny. If you were this poor mother hen you wouldn't have that grin on your face. No. As a good mother hen, I must teach you two to scratch for your food.

JOHN

(Scratches shoulders.) Like this?

JERRY

No. City boy. How could a duck scratch his shoulder? Ducks don't have shoulders. Ducks don't scratch at all. That's my problem. I try to show you like this **(Jerry scratches the desk with his foot)**. You do nothing. You just waddle on by.

(They walk by.)

No. Waddle like this.

(He demonstrates and they waddle. Jerry comes down from the desk.)

Next I must lead you past a pool of water. Follow me, waddling. Now you two turn into the water as little ducklings do.

(They turn and waddle in.)

Up goes my blood pressure. **(He runs around and around the "pool.")** They will drown. They will drown. Jesus, Mary and Joseph, and St. Anthony, save them, or they will drown. Now, sit. **(They sit on floor. He goes toward desk.)** No, not there. On the chairs. **(Jerry sits at desk.)**

JOHN

Yes.

JERRY

I am a good mother hen. Right?

SHARON

Yes.

JERRY

You are not bad ducklings, right?

JOHN

Hah. I guess not.

JERRY

Is it my fault there is a problem?

SHARON

No.

JERRY

Are you to blame for the problem?

SHARON

Nobody is to blame exactly.

JERRY

Not the poor mother hen.

SHARON

It's just a relationship problem. **(Half to herself, half to the audience.)** Wait a minute. Could that be all it was? Between me and Mam all those years. That's it. That is all it was. Nobody was to blame. Not Mam. Not me. How did he do that, John?

JOHN

How did he do what?

VOICE OFF STAGE

Someone is in your office, Doctor Kraus.

JERRY

Nothing to hide, silly people.

> (Dr. Kraus enters and comes down
> corridor to door and puts key in door. It

-149-

doesn't open. He knocks.)

DR. KRAUS

Anyone in there?

(Continues knocking. Jerry jumps up and goes out window as John unbolts the door.)

DR. KRAUS

Hello. How did you get in here? I am Dr. Kraus.

JOHN

The other doctor took care of us. **(Looks around.)**

DR. KRAUS

Oh, Dr. Carroll.

JOHN

We didn't get his name. He was here a minute ago.

SHARON

We thought he was you.

JOHN

We are the Helferns. We had a 2 o'clock appointment with you.

DR. KRAUS

(Phone rings.) We are having a bit of a tizzy here. A patient is missing. Excuse me. **(He answers phone and faces window.)** Hello. Oh thank heaven.

-150-

Yes, I can see him from here now in the garden. With a white coat on.

SHARON

(Half sings.) What did I tell you? I knew it.

JOHN

What?

SHARON

Jerry is the missing patient. I knew it.

JOHN

You know nothing.

SHARON

But I don't care. I don't care who he was. I feel light as a feather.

DR. KRAUS

He should be corrected immediately, James. Could you take care of it? Good. Tell him no more flower garden if he disappears again. Thanks much. (Hangs up.) We lost a patient while I was at lunch. Sorry I am late. (Looks at watch.) We won't have much time today but I can reschedule you.

JOHN

My wife doesn't want any more appointments after today.

DR. KRAUS

Oh? You don't want therapy?

-151-

SHARON

When could you reschedule me, Doctor?

DR. KRAUS

Let me see. **(Looks at book.)**

JOHN

Sharon, don't make an appointment you have no intention of keeping.

SHARON

Mornings if possible, Doctor.

DR. KRAUS

Mornings, let me see.

JOHN

Sharon, what is this?

SHARON

I'll shorten this coat and bring it next time. It's too long for you too.

DR. KRAUS

And you will?

SHARON

Sure.

DR. KRAUS

Well, his naughty behavior produced some good, didn't it? You said you wanted to make a morning appointment?

JOHN

Sharon, for heaven sake, what's going on here?

SHARON

It's all very simple, John. I didn't want to take therapy before. I thought it would put blame on my mother. But now I understand all that.

DR. KRAUS

I see. **(Pores over appointment book.)** Understand what?

SHARON

My mother was not to blame. Nor was I. It was chicken and duck. Good chicken and good duckling. Just a relationship problem between Mam and me. Nothing more.

DR. KRAUS

How about Wednesday morning?

JERRY

(Sticks head in window.) Sorry. I don't take morning appointments. **(Jerry exits.)**

DR. KRAUS

(Speaking out window, shaking finger.) Now Jerry Sands. Your behavior has been preposterous today. We will dig up that garden and sow weeds if you

don't behave. Now where were we? **(Looks in book.)** Wednesdays at 10:00.
OK?

SHARON

That will be fine, Doctor.

DR. KRAUS

Let's talk a little while anyway. There will be no charge, of course, for this
disaster today.

JOHN

Thank you very much, Doctor.

SHARON

Can patients receive money?

DR. KRAUS

Some can. We encourage responsibility.

SHARON

Can Jerry Sands?

DR. KRAUS

Yes.

SHARON

Let's give him his money, John.

-154-

JOHN

OK. How much, dear?

SHARON

Seven dollars and eighty-three cents. What else?

DR. KRAUS

$7.83? That's a rather strange number. Of course, numbers can be very significant.

SHARON

It's significant for me. I wouldn't be taking therapy except for Jerry.

JOHN

And that was his fee.

DR. KRAUS

Amazing. And amusing. Tell you what. In the spirit of things, I'll make my next fee $7.83 also.

SHARON

That is very generous of you, Doctor.

JOHN

Wait just one minute. A light just dawned on me.

SHARON

What's the matter, John?

JOHN

Wait just one cotton pickin' minute.

SHARON

What are you talking about?

JOHN

I want to see the manager of this place.

SHARON

What on earth for?

JOHN

I am not going to be made a fool out of. Not twice in one day. No siree.

SHARON

No one is making a fool of you.

JOHN

I am a mature man and nobody but nobody. ...

SHARON

Thank you very much, Doctor. We'd better go.

JOHN

I am going nowhere until I see that manager.

DR. KRAUS

Excuse me, please. **(Phone rings.)** I am a busy man. **(Answers phone.)** Yes
… yes.

JOHN

I don't care.

SHARON

John, what has gotten into you?

DR. KRAUS

May I call you back? Please.

JOHN

Can't you see anything? **(He counts on his fingers.)** One, he thinks this is
fun. Two, he is getting you to shorten the coat. Three, he is charging $7.83.

SHARON

So what?

JOHN

He's another nut, that's what. It's the same story all over. Another nut on our
hands.

DR. KRAUS

I must go. **(Hangs up.)** Will you please get out of this office?

SHARON

Don't be ridiculous, John. Please excuse this, Doctor.

JOHN

I'm not anybody's jackass.

DR. KRAUS

You could fool me.

JOHN

They are two peas in a pod. Do you see any difference in them?

SHARON

Of course. Be sensible. There are Dr. Kraus' diplomas.

JOHN

They were there for the other nut. I want pictures not diplomas.

DR. KRAUS

I must insist. Out please. I am cancelling your appointment.

SHARON

No. I want treatment.

DR. KRAUS

Well, take him out of here now.

JOHN

I have my rights as a mature person. I want to know who is who around here.

(Jerry comes in the window still wearing white coat.)

DR. KRAUS

(To Jerry.) What do you want? Out!

JERRY

(Delighted.) $7.83. I heard. I heard. I want to tell my mother the great news.

(Jerry picks up phone. Doctor tries to take phone from him. Jerry climbs up desk, taking phone out of reach of Doctor.)

DR. KRAUS

(Turns.) Are you still here! I am getting the security sergeant and emptying this office. Once and for all.

(Jerry dials phone.)

Get off that phone!

(Runs around the desk trying to catch phone from Jerry. Jerry on desk, eludes him.)

JOHN

Look at them. You tell me which one is which.

SHARON

Oh my God.

DR. KRAUS

(Starts out.) I am getting the sergeant and locking you all up. Trespassing....

SHARON

Please, let's talk like sensible adults.

DR. KRAUS

Show me one sensible adult!

SHARON

I want treatment. That's the number one. ...

DR. KRAUS

If you need treatment, what does he need? Mein gott in Himmel.

> (Dr. Kraus runs up corridor. John and Sharon follow, Sharon pleading, "Please, Doctor," as they all exit.)

JERRY

(Talking on phone while up on desk.) Hi Mam. Guess what! I made $7.83 today. ... Doctoring. ... Right, doctoring. With a white coat on. ... What's going on? Nothing much now. ... You can't speak to the Doctor. He ran out. A patient is chasing after him up the corridor. Don't forget to come Thursday. ... Today? You're coming this minute? See you, Mam.

(He hangs up and starts the same dance routine as before, repeating, "I am a dancing man.)
(Sharon, John and Dr. Kraus enter and come down corridor.)

JOHN

Anybody can make a mistake. Right?

(Jerry stops dancing and listens.)

Dr. KRAUS

All right. All right.

(Jerry bounds out the window as others enter office.)

JOHN

Even your Doctor Freudian was full of it some of the time.

DR. KRAUS

Some of the time. That's understandable.

JOHN

That's what I say.

DR. KRAUS

All right. Forget it all. We are here for the purpose of psychiatry. Not small talk. This is a Doctor's office. Now sit. Please. **(John and Sharon sit.)** I have patients scheduled. I must get back to normal.

JOHN

If anyone should try to be normal, you certainly. ...

SHARON

Shut up, John

DR. KRAUS

(Sits.) Now. **(To Sharon.)** Let's get started. You say you hate your mother?

(From facing Doctor, John and Sharon turn their heads slowly to face front.)

LIGHTS OUT

Acknowledgments

Thanks to the kindly dentists, Drs. Robert Gallagher and Stanley Ross, without whom I could neither smile nor speak to promote my book; to Marian Wilson, who patiently deciphered my scrawl and typed the manuscript; my friend and mentor, Aaron Elson, who helped this little book to see the light; and to Aaron's goddaughter, Avery Harken, whose graphic skills are evidenced by the front and back covers.

"

If I were to be blind after today, I would want to go off by myself in the mountain, climb to the highest cliff, and look out across the valley at the towns, farms and farmhouses.

I would want to picture each native tree in my mind, the rough bark and the shapely green leaves.

I would want to see the squirrels running and leaping from one walnut tree to another, and the birds flying.

I would like to see the deer run and jump swiftly and gracefully and leap across the fences, and lie in a tree that leans across the water and watch bass laying under the rocks and dart out after a fly.

I would go through the house from one room to the other picturing each piece of furniture, every corner and everything, in my mind.

I would like to see all my sisters, brother and parents together as we were, and picture each as they look for future reference.

I would want to see all my friends and relatives so I would know what the person looked like when I would talk to them after being blind.

I would want to go fishing and hunting and do the things I know I couldn't do after being blind.

– Billy Wolfe, Edinburg, Va., high school essay

Billy Wolfe, age 18
Killed in action
March 16, 1945
Pfaffenheck, Germany

WWII Oral History
www.tankbooks.com

Visit the World War II Oral History web site
www.tankbooks.com

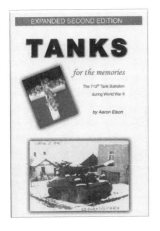
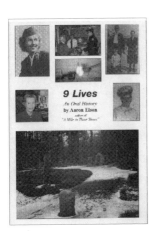